chapels or places of worship

~~places of worship~~ erected by the non-conformist sects. Such

~~monstrosities~~ ~~excrescences~~ one would think, can only be ~~temples~~ of ~~cant~~ and

nurseries *breeding cant turpitude*

~~humbug~~ ~~hypocrisy~~. There exist, ~~however~~, plain and unassuming little

still all the same, ... old-fashioned,

'Bethels', 'Zions' and 'Bethsedas', ~~which charm one by their atmosphere~~

dating from belonging to an earlier epoch, better epoch,

which charm one. ~~of simple piety.~~ *We used sometimes to be* ~~I enjoyed being~~ taken to *some of* these by our ~~Welsh~~

servants of a Sunday. The fervid singing, ~~the~~ praying, and ~~the~~

preaching, in a language, the more moving for being incompre-

powerfully

hensible, affected me ~~strangely~~, and when the orator broke into

the <u>hwyl</u> or afflatus, with which all Welsh sermons should

it sounded like

terminate. ~~I felt that I was listening to~~ the veritable voice

of God...

used to

We ~~would~~ visit ~~too~~ the home of our nurse, somewhere in the

wilds of ~~the~~ Precelly ~~hills~~. The men here were small, dark and

bearded. They were woodmen and probably Euskarians. Everybody

pointed

wore clogs with ~~pointed~~ brass toe-caps. We sat with our bowls

on our stools

dreamily in wonder

of <u>cawl</u> ~~before us~~ and listened, ~~as in a dream~~, to the ~~incessant~~

~~clatter of the clogs on the stone flags of the kitchen and~~ the

ceaseless Welsh bavardage of our friends.

~~tireless loquacity of our friends, few of whom knew a word of~~

~~English.~~

On market day t Haverfordwest the streets and squares were

full of life and movement. Noise too, with the continual lowing

of cattle, the screaming of pigs, and the loud vociferation of

the drovers. Among the crowd were to be seen the women of

Langum, in their distinctive and admirable costume, carrying

creels of the famous oysters on their backs. Tramps, looking

Finishing Touches

AUGUSTUS JOHN

Finishing Touches

edited and introduced by

DANIEL GEORGE

JONATHAN CAPE LIMITED
THIRTY BEDFORD SQUARE LONDON

ND
497
·J6
A2
1964

Printed in Great Britain
by Ebenezer Baylis and Son, Limited
The Trinity Press, Worcester, and London
on paper made by John Dickinson and Co. Ltd
Bound by A. W. Bain and Co. Ltd, London

Contents

The Illustrations

The frontispiece and numbers 5–15 are frames from the BBC Television film made at Fordingbridge for the series 'Face to Face', and are reproduced by kind permission of the Corporation. Number 2 is reproduced by permission of the late Sir David Low, and the self portraits by permission of Mrs John. Number 4 is the property of Mr George Rainbird who commissioned it in 1957 for the volume of fifty-two drawings which he published, and who kindly made it available for this book.

Introduction

IT WAS at Jonathan Cape's instigation, reinforced by a formal contract, that in the year 1938 Augustus John committed himself, not at all unwillingly, to the task of writing his memoirs. The idea of a chronologically ordered autobiography or continuous narrative soon had to be abandoned, anything like total recall proving to be beyond the memoirist's mnemonic capacity. Soon, too, the project itself had to be abandoned, or at least indefinitely postponed: the Second World War had intervened. The completion of the book and its publication being now so much in doubt, Jonathan, rightly deciding that such parts of it as had so far been written were too good to be denied the existing public and its posterity, arranged with Cyril Connolly for them to appear in *Horizon*.

With the coming, as we thought, of universal and perpetual peace, publisher and author resumed their business relationship. The book, it was agreed, should be finished with the minimum of delay. Augustus John seemed eager to take up his pen and write, but the products of his zeal were not forthcoming immediately, nor, after a brilliant if brief and tardy efflorescence, were they continued at a rate to bring publication day appreciably nearer. Secretarial assistance had been provided. What more was necessary to speed the starting writer? John Davenport, persona grata with the author, was enlisted as general encourager, and the two, it can be inferred, spent many pleasant days together at odd intervals. But progress with the written word still lagged behind schedule.

It was at this juncture that Jonathan proposed one of the pleasantest assignments of the many I undertook for him – undertook, in this case, I must add, with some reluctance, being well aware that I had not been gifted with the ingratiating manner, dominating personality or even resourceful unsnubbability of an efficient interrogator. Although not inexperienced at imparting confidence to commencing, nervous authors, or in applying spur or balm to established ones, I was inhibited by natural diffidence when dealing with men who had achieved fame outside the fields of literature. Who was I that I should succeed in wheedling Augustus John, busy with much more important things, into remembering his past, and not only remembering, committing the result to paper?

I need not have felt apprehensive. From the beginning, our association was a happy one, possibly because I was too respectful to be pertinacious, too shy to pry. Of his personal life I knew no more than what was more or less public knowledge; of his art about the same amount – what someone has called a useful smattering of ignorance. I had never mastered the critic's vocabulary: dispassionately I knew what I liked, what I didn't, and what I was indifferent to. Fortunately, Art with a capital A was not a subject on which this artist showed any inclination to hold forth. About his own painting he was not so much reticent as dismissive: 'What do you expect me to say? There it is, isn't it?' He would much rather talk about people, and sometimes the people got on to paper – not always; and what he wrote about them had to be closely scrutinized: it might be actionable if printed. His assurance that they were 'safely dead' had to be verified – often, as he put it, with unfortunate results: regrettably they were still alive. Not that he was ever malicious or vindictive: it was just that, the law of libel being what it is, publishers have to be cautious. Besides, I was not always satisfied that he had not conflated two or more people and as many incidents.

It must not be thought that I sat, notebook in hand, receiving an intarissable flow of reminiscence. A tape-recorder might have been of some use, but that was not at all the kind of business-like arrangement at which we arrived or ever wanted to. My function was merely that of the tactful prodder, the reminder of promises, the suggester of subjects, the gentle persuader. It was to be entirely his book, to be written in his own way, and – I was to find – at his own rate. He must not be hurried, certainly not goaded, into anything that went against his grain. Only, I politely insisted, he *must* get on with it. And, by fits and starts, he did. The fits were not frequent, and the starts soon became stops.

From time to time I would receive from him two or three quarto sheets of small beautifully formed and regular script, registered perfectly at the left-hand margin and with exactly equal distances between the long and economically spaced lines; but there were few lines without some alteration or insertion. On one such sheet now before me are twenty-five lines, only seven of which are without some emendation. One line reads: 'I am a devil for revision. I cannot write the simplest sentence without very soon thinking of a better one.' Here the words 'very soon' have been changed to 'at once'.

The trouble was that when his 'piece' had been typed and sent to him for retention, back it would come with further alterations and additions. (Alternatively, he would fail to return it and had to be reminded of his obligation.) Retyped and sent to him, it would reappear with still more corrections and interlineations. The process might have continued indefinitely had it not dawned on me, when he claimed credit for making progress, that he had forgotten earlier versions and was marking time instead of going forward. After that I 'forgot' to send him a copy including his second revisions; but he took full advantage of his opportunity when in extended due course he received the printed proof sheets.

We had many meetings but, after the first, no formal sitting, and even that first one did not go according to plan – *my* plan. On his invitation I visited him at Fryern Court. With his beret at what is known as a rakish angle and a bright scarf fluttering in the breeze, he was waiting for me at Salisbury railway station with a car (could it have been a Napier? No, not so old as that), which, I was a little alarmed to discover, he was determined to drive. In the town he had to stop for petrol. Asked by the attendant how much he wanted, he replied, 'Un bidon.' 'Nut?' said the attendant, looking at me and jerking his head in the direction of Augustus. Once through the town, we travelled at hearse-rate in the dusty rear of a column of infantry. 'No hurry,' I said, 'it's bad luck to pass troops on the march.'

We pulled up at a pub at which, judging by the landlord's greeting, he was no stranger. It was there that I was initiated into the mysteries of shove-ha'penny – or felt it incumbent on me as a guest to pretend such was the case. A foolish affectation; but I could never have beaten him at it. Thus delayed, we were late in reaching Fryern Court for lunch. Mrs John, unsurprised and uncomplaining, presided over a table at which – indeed *on* which – three or four cats joined us. 'Don't mind red wine with fish, do you?' said Augustus, filling a tumbler for me. Later I was glad to have it confirmed that I had seen a herd of white goats straying about the lawn.

After visiting the studio we settled down to business in a room which I might have described as a book-lined den if he hadn't once called me 'Book-lined Dan'. Business? Well, we talked and sometimes 'the book' was touched upon, but no *modus operandi* was established. He enjoyed writing it, calligraphically and compositionally, he said, and the process of recollection in tranquillity was fun; but how find leisure for this pastime? He was not in favour of sending me rough notes that I could interpret and 'style' for a secretary to copy, and I refrained from suggesting that I should brush up my self-taught shorthand and submit for his approval a report of our conversations. I was only too willing to agree that every word should be his own, in his own handwriting.

About three years were to pass before I received a copy of *Chiaroscuro* with the inscription in that exquisite handwriting, 'To Daniel George, without whom this book would still be unwritten – Augustus John.'

Does all this sound as though I were trying to take credit for a chance association in which the part I played in the production of a famous book was inconsiderable but generously exaggerated by the author? I shall be sorry to have given that impression. At the time it was little more for me than 'all in a day's work', but some particulars of that little more, it was supposed, might be of interest to readers of *Chiaroscuro* and this its sequel. That rather forbidding title was insisted upon by the author after many others – including *A Painter's Pastime* and *Many-Coloured Life* – had been discussed and dropped. It was not regarded by his publishers as a good title – difficult to pronounce, booksellers thought, as well as hard to understand. 'Not symbolically felicitous', I had ventured to say. But Augustus had evidently had his mind made up for him and was bored with the subject: *Chiaroscuro* it must be, with the concession of a subtitle, 'Fragments of Autobiography: First Series'. Later he was to have misgivings about it: 'I chose *Chiaroscuro* for its decorative value. Should one put underneath in brackets (Keeahroskooro) to guide the uninitiated?' He returned to its intimidating unfamiliarity years after: 'I have started a longer and more serious piece for my sequel to *Caroskero*, as an admirer pronounced it the other day.'

The book appeared in 1952, a handsome volume designed by G. Wren Howard, who has not forgotten the anxieties of selection and identification (especially of children in groups) when it came to the author's choice of illustrations, nor the trouble entailed by final instructions countermanded more than once. Moreover, changes made in the text of the already revised proof had done nothing to expedite delivery of the finished book from the printers.

Introduction

In the concoction of the blurb – the publisher's 'sales talk' printed on the jacket of the book – there had been spirited discussion, but the author was persuaded to withdraw his objections to what (since blurbs are perishable) seems just worth reproducing here:

> It was hardly to be expected that Augustus John would commit himself to writing a grave and formal autobiography: his lively intelligence and mercurial temperament forbid him to become either garrulously reminiscential or embarrassingly self-analytical. What began as a series of random recollections has – by expansion and contraction, by the process of one thing bringing up another, by the past welling up into the future and then subsiding – assumed a pattern which symbolizes and reveals the fruits of a long and unconventional life.
>
> Augustus John is already a legendary figure; it might be said that from his first descent upon London he has provided material for myth-makers, and that speculation what he would do next has never ceased. This book gives the substance of the legends. It is anecdotal and reflective; it is youthful; it is mature; entertaining and provocative; it is a work of literature by a great artist in another medium.

Re-reading it and remembering that it was intended to be a 'selling' blurb, I regard it as at least inoffensive in that it makes no extravagant claims and can hardly be thought misleading. Commercial considerations not neglected, it has, I submit, the merit of sincerity, though what was hoped to be conveyed by the bit about the pattern which symbolizes and reveals the fruits remains a little obscure.

Augustus was pleased with the Press reception of *Chiaroscuro,* while taking to heart such adverse criticism as lurked in the praise. 'Some people have complained,' he wrote later, 'that I do not treat at any length on the subject of Art. But naturally enough I have been put off by the immensity of the theme. In my next volume I intend to rectify this shortcoming to some extent and plunge boldly into a subject which the progress of modern archaeology widens every day. Without pontificating, of course, I can at least point out those manifestations of the creative faculty throughout the ages which must compel my homage if not my imitation.'

But this intention was not uppermost in his mind when I managed to get him started on 'Vol. Two', as we called it. The final section of *Chiaroscuro,* written with something of a flourish, was headed *Half Way House*: 'This must be about half way on my retrospective journey and high time to call a halt.' As a statement it was inexact: the author had obeyed no rule of chronology, made no attempt at continuity of narrative, and I had given up hope of inducing him to work to a system. At that moment he had had enough of 'pen-pushing', though having tasted ink, so to speak, he had no intention of becoming a total abstainer from it. But that was for the future. He resumed, as 'Vol. One' had ended, with a piece entitled 'Half Way House'. About the tone of this I was a little dubious. Was he in danger of becoming arch? Wasn't there a joke behind it, concealed from the general reader whom I represented? Was he perhaps hoping that he had implied something that he could later repudiate if necessary? He had stood a lot from me in the way of 'general reader's' criticism. If I offered any now, he might feel discouraged. 'Fine! Go ahead,' was all I could tell him. His later contributions, except for a few very much 'in character' hobbyhorse canters, conformed to his *Chiaroscuro* pattern of reminiscence, and I had no cause to blush when he wrote: 'I was so elated by your generous note that I felt moved

to add another piece and here it is. I hope you will find it up to
the mark: in any case your criticism will always be welcome.' It
wasn't always. But then it wasn't often expressed: there was no
occasion for it. He needed no instruction: what he deploringly
lacked was time and impetus.

To break a silence and, not without a guilty feeling that I was
distracting him from his real work, try to set him writing again,
I would sometimes send him a box of books, including, especially,
any bearing, however remotely, on 'his period' or any that
seemed likely to interest or provoke him to disagreement. I think
I here committed a tactical error: he was pleased to have the
books, and he made some sharp and not always complimentary
comments on the authors of them, but they must have invaded
his leisure while yielding little in the way of material for his
literary labour. Labour, I am afraid, it had become. Looking
through his letters I can spot only one instance of his admitting
that a book had been *useful*: 'I found Ken Tynan's book most
interesting and good; besides which it provided me with a useful
date, 1922, when I saw Granero wounded, to be killed the following Sunday. I can't call myself an *aficionado* in this connection,
but I find Tynan's way more sympathetic than Hemingway's.
I hope to send up some more stuff and nonsense against your
return ... ' He was entertained, for example, by Nina Epton's
The Valley of Pyrene and *Love and the French*, but I can't trace that
either induced him to resume authorship. The burden of his not
infrequent communications was apt to be: 'Perhaps I can now do
some more scribbling after a long break' – 'I hope to be seeing
you shortly. Will have a bit more of Vol. 2 to type but am busy
painting mostly' – 'I send you now a short piece for your consideration. I have been very much bogged in clay or would have
more to offer, but every little helps' – 'A fresh burst of energy in
the painting line has encroached on my inkpot but there is more
stuff simmering' – 'I am painting feverishly but without forget-

ting my literary responsibilities altogether' – 'I have had an accident. After conscientiously pruning an apple tree I slipped up and injured a leg which has had to be put in plaster and has immobilized me for over a week. It may be a week or two more before I can run about. In the meantime I read some of the books you sent ... Now while still somewhat crippled I shall get down to the book seriously and send you evidence of my industry soon' – 'I'm afraid I'm in your bad books again as I haven't sent you any fresh stuff for ages. The fact is I have been, and am, up to my ears in work – especially some rather enormous panels which I would like to show you. Can you not pay us another visit and bring Margaret some day soon?'

The last visit had been made by coach from Bournemouth, where my wife and I were spending a late holiday. Summoned to the telephone I was surprised to hear his voice – he had got my address from Jonathan. We must, he said, come to Fordingbridge; Dorelia would meet us half way, or at least at a convenient picking-up place. It was another pleasant occasion. Recently Jonathan Cape had been – I must not say complaining or chafing at the delay, but he was certainly beginning to despair of seeing 'Vol. Two' completed. 'Just tell him,' said Jonathan, 'that he's painted enough pictures. It's time he wrote a few books.' It seemed a good time to deliver this message. The response was: 'Tell Jonathan he's bought enough books – far too many. It's time he bought a few paintings.' Neither message had any visible effect.

I had been very careful not to badger or pursue him, and it seemed odd that when I stole away for a holiday he appeared anxious to get in touch with me. When – the year before or perhaps later – I was at Swanage he came over to see us with his daughter-in-law Simon, on whose portrait he was then, and had been for a long time, engaged. Meanwhile, from other people's memoirs, books of art criticism, and conversations with friends – Tommy Earp, Cynthia Asquith, John Rothenstein, and others – I had gleaned material for a few leading questions, but I cannot remember what they led to, not, anyhow, to long additional chapters.

We met fairly often – in my small backroom at No. 30 Bedford Square, at the Percy Street flat – or elsewhere in town for extended lunch or supper. An early lunch at the Monaco I recall because he there made an observation that piqued my curiosity. 'The last time I was in this place,' he said, 'I was thrown out of it.' Naturally I asked 'Why?' and 'Who were you with?' No answer to either question. 'Oh, come, don't clam up on me,' I protested, but he vouchsafed no more. There was a mischievous twinkle in his eye – a signal I had learned to recognize: if I pressed him he was capable of replying, 'I'd come to blows with the Archbishop of Canterbury.' (That twinkle in his eye gets into his prose, so does his barely audible chuckle, but his sudden loud sardonic laugh has been kept right out of it, only the delayed smile of the *moqueur* surviving as a visual image.)

I was always cautious in questioning him, if only because once in a letter he had said: 'People have asked me for further reminiscences of early days on which I have only touched so far. I know that I have disappointed many by my evasion of the more "lurid" aspects of my life so far, and I did so deliberately, as I don't feel at all "lurid" and would like to stifle this myth together with the cheap journalists who have given it currency. I think I may say that I have been consistently innocent on the whole and not least when engaged in the scandalous activities imputed to me which if they were founded on fact must have been as enjoyable as they are unprintable.' This letter ends: 'I read Caitlin Thomas's book. As a self-portrait it's an absolute knock-out. Unlike me, she cannot avoid the truth even at its ghastliest.' Earlier he had complained that in America *Chiaroscuro* had been advertised as by a *bon vivant* and a gossip columnist: 'I don't consider myself either, and have told Higham [his literary agent] to let them know that

18

I find such remarks injurious and uncalled for.' His fierce objection to being presented as living up to the legend would have daunted me had I ever been tempted to play the delicate prober. My reiterated ironical 'Come, throw discretion to the winds!' might amuse him, but failed to induce expansiveness on paper.

We were at the Monaco together only once. A restaurant we frequented regularly was the White Tower, about which he had written in a reminiscence of its earlier days as the Eiffel Tower under the proprietorship of Rudolf Stulick, and at which he now felt at home under John Stais, who could always find a table for us. Dorelia joined us there on one occasion, I very well remember. Sloane Square is a far cry from Bedford Square for lunch, but while Augustus had a studio in Chelsea it was at the Queen's restaurant, just inside Cliveden Place, that we often met. There were times when conversation was a little restricted: he would become detached from his deaf-aid, or its battery would die on him, and he seemed unaware that anything was wrong. Or he may have enjoyed the spectacle of my mouthing soundlessly, audible though my raised voice must have been six tables away. (Dorelia once hinted that his deafness was optional: he could often hear when he wasn't intended to.) But his hardness of hearing was no real handicap to either of us; otherwise our meal-time colloquies would not have been so prolonged. At Bertorelli's he was always made much of. When we were last there it was for a very late sitting. Everyone else had left and chairs were piled on tables when the amiable *patron* joined us. It had passed midnight when I accompanied Augustus up the steep stairs of his daughter's flat in Percy Street.

In these conversations something said would activate the cells of his memory, and, if my own memory rose to the occasion, I would write to remind him of his recollection and extract a further instalment from him. The experiment was never tried, but I have good reason for doubting whether his cells could have been, like Proust's, stirred into activity by a *madeleine* dunked in tea; and I was no Boswell to record his table-talk. But little by little, the material for 'Vol. Two' accumulated – still not enough for Jonathan's requirements and far short of the amount he so keenly desired to write, or indeed of the amount he had managed to persuade himself he had written: it always surprised and disappointed him to learn that it wasn't much larger. Repetition sometimes crept in and tact was needed in drawing attention to it. He was not to be nagged, nor did he respond to badinage on a subject which he had every right to take seriously. An attempted pleasantry of mine to the effect that I hoped he would not use the open spaces of 'Vol. Two' for gypsy encampments was not a success; and the stoniest of silences was opposed to my polite rendering of Jonathan Cape's injunction, 'Tell him to pipe down on politics.' From the free expressions of his views on current Home and Foreign Affairs he was by no means deterred by the remark of one reviewer of *Chiaroscuro* (I think John Davenport) that Augustus John was the only anarchist with the Order of Merit. He left much unwritten. He had much to say; some of it he found difficulty in expressing in the individual style he had evolved, but what he succeeded in putting into writing, with what he clearly if obliquely implied, entitles him to be classed with the artist-philosophers – a distinction he would have disdained.

To encourage him by ensuring that some of his later writings saw the light of print I was able to engage the interest of John Lehmann, editor of *The London Magazine*, who was delighted to accept a selection for publication; and in 1958 Leonard Russell of *The Sunday Times* made a brave show with the series of 'Candid Impressions'. The attention these attracted acted as a useful stimulus to the author, but it was soon spent – no, the truth is rather that he could not find time or opportunity to reduce to writing all the memories and ideas with which his mind was teeming.

He was a 'Sunday writer' in the sense that some men are 'Sunday painters', but he had too few free Sundays.

*   *   *

Imposition of noticeable continuity on these further 'fragments of autobiography' was thought neither feasible nor desirable. An arrangement of them in groups that the author might himself have linked – it was his often-expressed intention of 'putting the stuff in order' – was as much as I felt justified in attempting. Should it still be thought that I have exceeded my editorial duties by writing this Introduction, I shall protest that its object is not to inflate the trouble I took, or was put to, in trying to bring the book to publication point, but solely to emphasize the fact that it was written at intervals in a busy life, against obstacles of all kinds, myself perhaps forming one of them.

For what Augustus John has bequeathed us from his excursion into the craft of letters we can feel grateful while wishing it more: it is not, in bulk alone, an inconsiderable legacy. Of its value as an autobiographical document and an addition to the history of art I leave others to form an estimate.

DANIEL GEORGE

Half Way House

THE above heading must not be taken as indicating my actual situation, which of course lies much further ahead; but I use it as a convenient metaphor, since from this point, before I reach the dark barrier ahead of me, I have as far to go again, in retrospect I mean. This barrier I mention is the Virgin Forest I must traverse if I am to gain those distant heights I see above the tree-tops: would these be the Delectable Mountains of which another traveller has told, and can that be Beulah-land I see beyond? I wonder ...

*   *   *

The Inn is closed, and though refreshed I am in no hurry to take the road. I sink into a bed of heather and dream. In my dream I seem to stand at the end of a long gallery, of which the windows on one side are hung with tattered curtains and some are boarded up; but through a few of them the light shines unimpeded, to illuminate a series of tapestries upon the opposite wall. The designer of these, it would seem, under a more powerful compulsion than mere obedience to the accepted rules of good taste, but rather as if inspired by the whispered adjurations of a private demon, has assembled elements of a surprising incongruity, which perplex when they do not offend the beholder; and yet at a certain distance they resolve themselves into a consistent and harmonious pattern. In one panel Beauty smiles derisively in the embrace of Satyrs, while Homeliness, gathering her skirts, prostrates herself before the throne of Eros. In another, old men are observed to dance together, but the young, disdaining pleasure, seek to climb impossible cliffs. Here, issuing from a crowd of drunken peasants, a Fairy bounds into the air, and with her starred wand imposes upon all her Empire of Illusion, while at the same time a professional clown, made up in the likeness of Divinity, pokes his head through the sky and winks ... Children without the least sense of propriety disport themselves everywhere. The landscape, consisting mostly of brown paper rocks, is decorated with dwarfed trees bearing preposterous flowers, and, above, diaphanous clouds swim like fish in a pond. Many of the compositions are unfinished or partly rubbed out, but all strike me somehow as vaguely familiar, as if I had been there before sometime ... long ago ...

*   *   *

To change the slide:

I find myself in a dusty lumber room, seeking treasure where it is least likely to be hidden. In a corner I come upon a decrepit bureau. Pulling out an obviously secret drawer, a packet of old letters and picture postcards and post-dated cheques is disclosed. These may be worth looking through, for I must have once considered them worth keeping; perhaps a few of them may still have interest and will help to fill a gap or two in this hotch-potch, or by association revive old memories upon which to draw, for the purposes of what it pleases me to call my

Magic Lantern Show

Behold a youth setting forth into the world to earn a living. He carries a portfolio and a small case to hold his few necessities; a copy of Shakespeare's *Hamlet* is included among these. From time to time he stops, consults this volume as if it were a guide book, and then proceeds more resolutely on his way. Who can it be? Reader, not to deceive you, this youth is, was, or will be myself ... I had been commissioned to do two drawings through the intermediation of a fashionable lady of Hampstead whose husband's acquaintance I had made. Before going further, I will give a short account of the circumstances of this young man's brief appearance on the stage I sometimes trod myself. George, for that was his name, was, it was generally agreed, on the threshold of a brilliant career. In addition to his native gifts enhanced by academic training, he was understood to be well connected and to have great expectations. How he and Will Rothenstein had come together I do not know, but no doubt the attraction was mutual.

Rothenstein at that time was living in Church Row, Hampstead, where he and his wife Alice were in the habit of entertaining a small elite of writers and artists of their acquaintance. Among the habitués usually to be seen at the time I am speaking of were Joseph Conrad, Cunningham Grahame, W. H. Hudson, and sometimes W. B. Yeats, if not George Moore himself. These stood for Literature. Art, or more precisely the New English Art Club, would be represented by Wilson Steer, Henry Tonks, Charles Conder and Walter Sickert and our host himself, while as odd man out Max Beerbohm, although he misrepresented everybody, was claimed and acclaimed by both sections.

These symposiums were notable for a discreet cheerfulness. It was as if the participants had been able to bring with them only a moderate provision of good spirits, which, in order to last out the evening, needed careful husbanding. If Cunningham Grahame were inspired to contribute one or two of his funny Scottish stories, he could be depended upon to clothe them decently under an impenetrable layer of dialect. There might be ladies present ... There was always Alice Rothenstein. Her comprehensive smile seemed to entoil everybody in a common enchantment. This was the nearest we got to intoxication, for our host's rule of austerity prohibited any closer approach. Aware of this, I used sometimes to visit The King of Bohemia on my way up the hill. The name of this pub attracted me powerfully and its magic was not belied by the quality of the liquor to be obtained within. Thus, after a salutary draught or two, I arrived to face the refinements of Church Row in better fettle, though sometimes a little late.

Rothenstein's new recruit, though only just recovering from the nervous breakdown following his recent marriage, seemed to enjoy the fresh and easy-going character of these gatherings, an atmosphere no doubt very different from the climatic conditions of the homelife to which he was as yet uninured. Under the stimulus of Will's tireless ebullience, which however did not conceal an undercurrent of seriousness (in the passage of years to become more and more marked), he began to expand and blossom forth himself, in a style combining scholarship with an attractive diffidence and humour. He felt perhaps that here was a means of escape from the insidious encroachments of domesticity, and accordingly attached himself to Will Rothenstein with the desperate haste of a man caught in the quicksands. This led to close intimacy, but never, I believe, to any relationship exceeding the bounds of propriety. The liaison was of the spirit. Will, on his part always on the lookout for signs of intelligence, especially in his admirers, took George, so to speak, to his bosom, and constituting himself his mentor and guide, put him to forced marches on the Heath, but only under the closest supervision. This discipline, which might have suited a taller and stronger man, soon began to tell on the novice, who, sadly out of training, found himself out-classed at all points, with his toes, his morale and his mental equilibrium all in danger. As he gave ground under the pressure of Will's dialectic, their progress began to take on the form of a succession of spirals (in imitation it would seem of the upward flight of the greater birds), allowing me from my station in the background to regain, by a short cut, contact at each point of intersection: but I soon fell comfortably behind ... On such occasions Will was at his most formidable. Released from the difficulties of painting, of which he so often complained, his spirit was free to soar beyond the reach of an intractable brush and the maddening problems of light, into regions of pure speculation, whence he would look down on struggling humanity as from the top of a tower; not, it is true, with the majestic calm of his friend Rabindranath Tagore, but with the understanding, tolerance and humour of one who had himself, as the saying is 'been through it'.

Life, golden and mysterious Life, was ever the object of this Prospector's quest. The mastery of Life! Was not that after all the ultimate meaning of Philosophy? Even Art came second to this, and Business, of course, only third.

Sad indeed for all who knew him was George's untimely collapse under Will Rothenstein's tutelage; but the tragedy fell, I fancy, most heavily on the senior partner in an association which meant so much to him in the present and promised so much more in the future. Alas! Now no longer could he envisage with complacence the hour he was preparing for, when, his task ended, he could safely hand over his Torch to the beloved disciple and so, turning his face to the wall, murmur his *Nunc Dimittis* like a Christian ...

To return to the drawings. The work I had undertaken meant a journey to the west of England. My first stopping-place proved to be a magnificent house standing in a great park. The lady of the house (who was to be my model) received me graciously and with an absent-minded gesture poured me out a cocktail. I was at once struck, even awestruck, by her beauty, but was just saved from complete intimidation by an air of naivety which, I think, almost matched my own. A pretty young girl at her side greeted me, too, but without warmth. Perhaps she held the old-fashioned view that artists should be kept in the kitchen when not at work. If this was the case, I was inclined to agree with her. Dinner that evening I found, like all the subsequent meals, was a gloomy business. An atmosphere of excruciating boredom seemed to pervade the whole establishment.

Next day I commenced my drawing, and after two or three sittings produced something which I thought passable, and which elicited the languid approval of its subject. Before leaving this house I was taken upstairs by my sitter and shown a private chapel she had contrived under the roof. This was pretty but not, I thought, quite convincing. Perhaps in the absence of a husband who, it appeared, was always away – shooting – life in this remote place had its dull hours and so the lady took to a mild form of religiosity as a means of lightening the little cloud of melancholy which hung about her, and which, in my opinion, only added to her charm. Within the wall of her sanctuary I noticed a recess which, at a glance, might have been a boudoir or a confessional – or both; but I had no time to investigate this feature, for I had now to move on to my next assignment. Here I found myself in similar surroundings but in an atmosphere less tense with hidden drama. My new hostess was no less amiable than the first, but kept no supercilious girl at her side, nor did she betray any symptoms of the 'blues', but she had one thing at least in common with the other, in that her husband, too, was away – shooting ... The drawing done, I returned to London with two cheques in my pocket. These were perhaps my first professional earnings, but I was the richer in more ways than one.

A Bang on the Head

W HILE I was a student at the Slade an event occurred to which was attributed undue importance at the time. It may now prove amusing to recall it. I had returned to Tenby for the summer holidays. I might have been about sixteen years old. One day my father and I took a walk along the beach to Giltar Point. I intended to bathe and took a towel with me. The tide was far out, but on the turn. Exploring this unaccustomed bathing place, I found a rock which offered, I thought, a good take-off. The water below appeared to be deep enough for a dive, but was by no means clear, the surface being encumbered with seaweed. Still, taking a chance, I stripped and made the plunge. Instantly I was made aware of my folly. The impact of my skull on a hidden rock was terrific. The universe seemed to explode! Yet I wasn't stunned. Perhaps the cold water saved me for I was able to get out of it, replace the flap of scalp I found hanging over one eye, tie the towel round my head, dress and rejoin my father, who was much alarmed by my plight. We made for home as fast as we could, but did not take the nearest way up the cliff, for that would have probably meant publicity which was at all costs to be avoided, but we ascended by zigzag steps further on, which permitted us to cross the Esplanade quickly and gain our house beyond more discreetly. I was feeling now decidedly weak and went to bed to await the doctor. When he arrived I was surprised and pleased to recognize, not our usual practitioner, but Dr Lock, a much more exciting personage. I had often admired him as he drove past in his smart gig, attired for the occasion in a style as sportive as it was appropriate, or on foot taking his 'old-fashioned' sheepdogs for a run. He had a strong handsome face and looked superb and perhaps a trifle haughty in his loneliness, for I never saw him in company. Could he have been under some cloud? I wondered. Certainly there was gossip. From what I overheard, this gentleman had been involved in an affair of the heart, which actually culminated in an elopement, but not a very serious one (which made it all the worse), for the fugitives got only as far as the next village, where, on second thoughts, they decided to renounce the project and return, the lady to her teeming family, the doctor to his dogs. This reasonable Don Juan was now engaged in thrusting an apparently very blunt needle through my scalp, an uncommonly thick one, it appeared (a circumstance to which I probably owed my life). The stitches held, there was no concussion, and in due course I was discharged cured and returned to the Slade, wearing, to conceal my wound, an out-of-date smoking-cap of black velvet with gold embroidery, produced by my father. My entry into the life room thus attired caused a sensation which my subsequent performances with a stick of charcoal only increased: and thus was born the myth of my *genius*, due, it seemed clear, solely to the bang on the head I had incurred while bathing. This, it was thought, had released hidden and unsuspected springs ... It was all nonsense of course; I was in no way changed, unless my fitful industry with its incessant setbacks, my wool-gathering and squandering of time, my emotional ups and downs and general inconsequence can be charitably imputed to that mishap.

* * *

It was time to leave the Slade and set up as a real artist. As Evans and McEvoy were just as hard up as I was, we decided to club together and take a studio in Charlotte Street, and as we couldn't afford models we sometimes posed for each other. This studio was quite small, too small in fact for three students, but we spent a good deal of time roaming about the town with our sketch books. In the evenings, whenever we could afford it, we went to the music halls. On Sundays, when I was usually alone, I often used to go to Hyde Park and listen to the orators and watch the people. There was to be found then a far greater variety of character than can be met with now. What must have been the last tattered remnants of the Strolling Players would give performances of an Elizabethan crudity and charm, while amidst the crowd philosophers would engage in subtle disputation. Wisdom rubbed shoulders with buffoonery; heresy with orthodoxy; the sacred with the profane. But all this was long ago, before the bobbies had cleaned up our civilization and forced us to be good.

I used sometimes to paint all night. The landlady informed my friends that she had been awakened one night at about four o'clock in the morning by vague noises. She got up, lit a candle and explored; seeing a light under my door she entered, to find me at work. 'Oh, Mrs MacGilliveray,' I had said with simplicity. 'I'm painting my Adam and Eve!' ...

My next move was to Albany Street near Regent's Park. The studio here was lit by a skylight and resembled a ship's cabin except for the absence of port-holes. I had it all to myself. The landlord was French and so was his wife, who was young, beautiful and had golden hair. I saw little of her till she came to me one day in great distress, weeping, for she was in deadly fear of her elderly husband, who, she said, might beat her to death. But what on earth could I do about it? The husband next confronted me, hopping mad. I don't know what he said. He was quite inarticulate. I don't know what I said either, but at least I kept calm. At last he took himself off, though still spluttering. Never have I met such a flagrant case of outraged impotence! I pitied his young wife, and perhaps, if I had had money, I would have taken her away to safety. In any case, that I think is what I ought to have done. But soon after I left the studio, and with regret lost sight of this ill-matched but interesting couple.

The Girl with the Flaming Hair

IN QUEST of a model, I made the acquaintance of a young woman late at night in Tottenham Court Road. She had hair of flaming red which contrasted, I thought pleasingly, with her pale mask of a face. She appeared to have no regular work, and readily agreed to sit for me. Uneducated, her conversation was somewhat rustic, but it was unaffected, original and often humorous. We became quite friendly as the work progressed. Such was her good nature that, though God knows poor enough herself, she would sometimes offer me a pound or two if she thought I needed it.

One morning, during my temporary absence, my model dropped off to sleep on the divan. On returning I received a severe shock. There lay the familar figure, but something terrifying had happened to it. The head seemed to have been replaced by a barber's pole, hairless, featureless, and in this connection horrible beyond words. Cerebrating wildly, I had to dismiss the idea of a practical joke. There could have been no substitution. I kept no lay-figure in the studio. As I gazed round in my perplexity, I quickly discovered the explanation. There, half hidden on the floor by the divan, gleamed the ruddy locks of my model's chevelure, her chief, perhaps her only glory ... After all, then, it was only a wig, which becoming detached, had fallen while its owner turned face downwards in her sleep, thus exhibiting the gratuitous indecency of a denuded occiput.

Great was my disillusionment. A judicious touch of the toe, followed by hasty retreat, sufficed to bring the sleeper to her senses, and on my re-entry after a few minutes I found her awake and smiling, and busy with the arrangement of her hair which had naturally got a little tousled.

Though my model was now looking her best again, I felt strangely loth to continue my work that day. Perhaps the state of my nervous system, overwrought by what had passed, precluded that moral detachment and calm which my work required. I could not blind myself to the difficulties now facing me. How, to begin with, could I hope to dissimulate successfully my knowledge of the awkward secret? Why, indeed, should it be necessary to do so? After all, congenital baldness is no crime, neither is it anything catching; it is merely unusual. Should it not be accepted frankly, and, among friends ar least, with humour? Considering the susceptibilities of a girl dependent wholly for a living on her appearance, I knew this was impossible. But equally impossible was an association based on misunderstanding and deceit. Without doubt, the young woman would continue naively to keep up a pretence, which, by an unlucky chance and without her knowledge, had been laid bare, thus giving rise to a cruel and ridiculous situation, which no show of dignity on her part or innocence on mine, could possibly save, or even fail to intensify. No! I couldn't trust myself to take part in such a farce. Rather than court failure and the certainty of eventual discomfort for both of us, I more wisely dismissed my young friend and turned her unfinished picture to the wall.

A Visit to Picton Castle

AT A DATE unspecified, I found myself staying at Picton Castle, near Haverfordwest. My host, Sir John Phillips, Lord Lieutenant of the County and a sympathetic young man, was no stickler for formality and left me free to rove, for I was bent on exploration. Here, at what might be called the centre of Pembrokeshire, I felt at home, in the widest sense, since it was in this vicinity that my dim ancestors first emerged from anonymity; here, on or under the flanks of Precelly Top (our Celtic Venusberg), might, I thought, be found some clue to my true origin, a secret, as it seemed to me, too jealously guarded by my respected but un-communicative parent (if indeed he was aware of it). I was dis-appointed by such few glimpses as had been afforded me of our more recent family history. The annals of mediocrity, even if carefully bowdlerized, fail as a source of inspiration, and I was never attempted by them to cultivate a restrospective ambition. Rather am I apt to search much further back than human memory can tell of, to Pre-history and the Dawn, for clues to a clearer sense of personal identity, and some fellow-feeling to go with it.

The megalithic monuments which are found on the Precelly range have always aroused in me, besides the normal reactions of surprise, curiosity and awe, some stranger sense of recognition, as if I had seen and known them already, some time long ago ... However, not being an archaeologist, I must leave the mystery of the stones for my friends Professor Stuart Piggott, Sir Mortimer Wheeler and others to investigate, if they have not already done so. For the time being I must be content to gaze and wonder. We know the famous blue stones of Stonehenge have been imported (like me) from Precelly, for (again like me) they are found nowhere else. These are sacred stones and Precelly is a sacred mountain, facts which provide another reason why I should feel an attachment to it, though its delicate profile forming the apex to the county, together with the long contours of its subsidiary ridges, are of themselves quite beautiful enough to ensure devotion.

'Know thyself,' said the sage: by all means, but for this some introduction seems necessary. Who *am* I in the first place? The answer is not so easy and may take the form only of a rough and ready approximation to the truth. The elements composing the population I belong to are so many and various as to make precision impossible. 'A Pembrokeshire Man' will have to do, since the definition briefly and happily summarizes the proud resultant of a multitude of ethnic strains, each in turn claiming precedence in a community permanently and geographically split by language and further fragmented by religious, political, cultural and sartorial differences. The chief line of division (linguistic) passes through Haverfordwest, where, on a market day, one may hear English spoken on one side of the High Street and Welsh on the other, with a mixture of both in the middle.

It was to this capital town that I would first repair of a morning, for my car might need petrol, oil, or a look-over. The garage was conveniently placed on an open space, or square, on the other side of which stood what was formerly the Salutation Hotel. It is now called the County Hotel, but cannot be said to live up to all that title usually implies. At some previous date the old Salutation, coming under new management, had been subjected to the irresistable march of progress, and at the hands of a gang of painters, plumbers, carpenters and plasterers, quickly transformed into a very fair imitation of a popular sea-side tea-shop or café. The result, however dainty and refined, was untraditional, and, taking into account the character of the clientele, inharmonious. The public, in spite of the new splendour, persisted in remaining unresponsive to the appeal of art and

35

aluminium, and, wonderful to relate, it was the *new look* which first gave way, not the customers! Obdurate in their basic conservatism, these callous but necessary drinkers were proof against the allurements of modernity, while, before their indifferent eyes, the paint peeled off, the plaster cracked and the spurious metal wilted!

At the rear of the establishment, however, I found a large bar, so faintly illuminated as to leave all modern improvements, at whatever stage of decay, mercifully in the shade. But behind the counter, dramatically, a young lady serving seemed to gather to herself such beams of light as succeeded in penetrating the wholesome gloom reigning elsewhere, while at her back a generous supply of bottles reflected them in gleams of liquid gold. This Hebe's colouration at once revealed her origin: its Rubenesque quality could only have derived from Flanders, and – more immediately – from the village of Langwm down the river, where flourishes to this day the last authentic remnant of the Flemish settlement. I am now voicing the popular belief; but, as a matter of fact, we know that a pure racial type can, and often does, reappear after generations of reckless cross-breeding; and as for the Flemings, their descendants are to be detected everywhere in the southern part of the county.

Sometimes, while I brooded alone in the half light of this bar, a group of young fellows might come in for a drink; brave, good-looking boys with tousled hair, cheap clothes and easy manners, they would now and then vary their conversation with a short burst of song. This seemed quite usual here and surprised nobody. Their jokes, to a stranger, might sound obscene, but at any rate they clearly owed nothing to metropolitan standards of humour and personally I found them none the less acceptable for that.

At last, after failing to decide on any particular itinerary, I would bestir myself with an effort, recapture my car, and make for the coast, where I found the lovely shores of Broad Haven decorated by innumerable black turds. It looked as if an International Peace Conference had taken place here, but at the lowest level.

The last time that I had visited Haverfordwest, as a small boy in my father's company, we lunched at the Salutation accompanied by a gentleman with whom the lawyer had much to talk about. I was left out of this conversation, since, as it consisted entirely of local gossip, I was out of my depth and could contribute nothing of value. The discussion ended in a dispute. Was a certain person, known to both, dead or alive? That was the question. My father insisted on the former contingency; his friend, more quietly, on the latter. There could be no possibility of compromise here. At last, neither party giving way, we left to catch our train back to Tenby, my father being visibly elated at what he foresaw would be one up to him, and was banking on his opponent's discomfiture, when the truth became known beyond a doubt. But on the way a poster arrested his attention. The announcement contained clear evidence that the subject of the recent disagreement was quite alive and active. My father was greatly agitated. He had committed a serious bloomer. 'I must go back and apologize,' he said. So back we hurried and found his friend still at the table. The *amende honorable* was received good-humouredly and the incident closed. But we missed our train.

I think this rather painful object-lesson in good (and bad) manners was worth more than any number of copy-book maxims. My father's attitude had been overweening but in the end his sense of correctitude prevailed. He acted properly at some inconvenience and saved his honour.

Near Picton Castle stands Slebech Hall. It is a tall, tower-like house, designed perhaps by one of the Adam brothers. It seemed to be derelict and there was nothing to stop me going in, for the door was open. I found the principal room had been decorated by frescoes of a more than Pompeiian lubricity. These spirited though ephemeral productions were no doubt the work of a soldier, for I learnt that the house had been occupied by the military. The artist had seen the possibilities of these spacious walls, and had certainly let himself go. I, too, felt my imagination stir as I explored the interior. The house was empty and neglected. Could I not somehow get hold of it? In the wilderness below a ruined church thrust a broken arch above the trees, and further down a fine and well-kept vegetable garden followed the left bank of the River Cleddan for some hundred yards or more up stream. Upon inquiry I was informed by my host that Slebech belonged to his sister, who, he said, didn't use it and no doubt would let me have it for nothing – especially if I would draw her portrait. How excited I was to hear this! How wonderful to have at last what I had so often dreamed of, a foothold in the heart of my own country; nay, much more than a foothold, a place in which I could work, and a kind of ivory tower in an enchanting ambience from which I would never want to stir and where there was room for all my dreams to come true!

But tragedy rudely intervened: poor Johnny Phillips died in his bath. The drawing was never done and Slebech Hall was sold.

Some say one should be indifferent to one's surroundings: but how is that possible except to an architect, an idiot or an anchorite?

Fitzroy Street

FLEAS or no fleas, the Fitzroy Quarter in those days was in every way much livelier than it is now. It was cosmopolitan, of course, with French and German elements predominating, but every other form of low life abounded. Living was cheap, according to modern standards, and the restaurateurs humane.

It was still the Artists' Quarter, its only rival being Chelsea. Its numerous studios, especially when they were 'To Let', bore witness to a long-standing picture-making industry, going back to Constable, and further. Some of them still housed a few exhausted survivors of the Pre-Raphaelite age. Had not Ford Madox Brown inhabited the haunted house with the big stone vase in Fitzroy Square? Other sky-lights illuminated the last feeble convulsions of the Neo-Classical revival whose princely leader, Leighton, had built himself a palace – and a tomb – in a more respectable district. But in my time, figures no less illustrious, though alive and sometimes kicking, were to be met with in the street. Here I renewed my acquaintance with James McNeil Whistler, whom I found most polite. I mentioned Ida Nettleship, who had been his pupil in Paris, had posed for him and was now my wife. Mr Whistler spoke of her with much sympathy, asking me to make her his compliments, then, raising his black straw hat, proceeded on his way to a French restaurant, where he was due for a one-and-sixpenny luncheon: he never paid more. Walter Sickert, too, was a neighbour, although somewhat intermittently, for he frequently changed his address. Ida and I had installed ourselves in the top floor of No. 95. I had a small studio at the back. Next door McMurdo and Selwyn Image kept a kind of Post-Pre-Raphaelite stronghold. Sometimes the tall grave figure of Sturge Moore, crowned by a large gardener's straw hat, would be seen to issue from this abode; but whoever might appear, nobody could hold me when there was music in the air: and not the music of Arnold Dolmetsch either, but something of a more popular kind from up the street. The source of this was a piano organ, manipulated by a young man with a painted face and dressed in motley. A young girl in a ballet skirt and tights danced vigorously to the music, while a third bedizened member of the band rushed hither and thither among the audience, extending an inverted clown's hat to all within hearing.

These strollers were not unknown to me. I often saw them. I used to get the ballerina to pose for me. Those flashing eyes, that swart mongolian face (the nose seemed to have been artificially flattened), framed in a halo of dark curls, made an impression not to be shaken off lightly. I had been reading Heine with delight and his *Florentine Nights* had helped to condition me for such encounters, to which, in any case, I wasn't at all unresponsive by nature.

Opposite No. 95 was Thackeray House, or 'The Newcomes', where laboured Herbert Everitt, son of my evangelical friend Augusta Stewart Everitt, who now kept a boarding house at Swanage.

Everitt's studio, littered with trophies from the tropics, bore witness to his extensive voyages. Sailing was his passion and the ocean the eternal setting for his top-heavy windjammers. Whatever might be said of these stately craft, nobody could dispute the artist's exact disposal of every rope of their complicated rigging.

A Dublin Affair

WILLIAM ORPEN had a cavernous studio in the basement of the same house, where he once painted a most regrettable portrait of me. Having selected Whistler's 'Carlyle' for imitation, he posed me seated in profile against the wall, attired in a cast-off top-coat provided by Charles Conder. Unfortunately the result of his industry revealed no trace of the subtlety and distinction present in his exemplar. Nor, considered as portraiture, could it be said to communicate the least hint of the shy, dreamy and reticent character of his model. It has been said that the greatest portraitists, at their most inspired, in some mysterious way imbue their subject with some reflection of their own personality, so that the least noteworthy or ambitious sitter gains, by the magic of Art, a nobility and refinement hitherto unsuspected by his friends, and only perhaps dreamt of by himself. If this is so, the picture in question must be considered as an unhappy illustration of a reversal of this process, for in this case the artist in degrading his model has betrayed himself. Our physical dissimilarities were such as to admit of no confusion: we could not be said to overlap in any way; in short, we had nothing in common but our psychological differences. But such a division, in its nature incomplete, will still permit of a limited degree of contact, nor, while it holds, need it prohibit the indulgence of light play, excusable at any rate among the young of whatever species.

A visit to the zoo will be enough to convince anybody of the truth of these observations, for here, and more especially in the monkey house, we may watch the association of elements ordinarily incompatible but now united by the limitations of a common barrier.

Talking of zoos, Orpen gave me the following account of an

episode at the Dublin Zoo, in which he figured honourably enough. It appears that as a student he was in the habit of visiting the zoo for the purpose of sketching the animals. One day, he was sketching a large anthropoid ape when he was surprised by this creature's behaviour. It would approach as near as the bars of the cage permitted, and, stretching out its arm, endeavour to divert the attention of the young artist, but without malice, while at the same time uttering soft, conciliatory sounds. Orpen, touched by these overtures, and perhaps a little flattered, responded with a smile and a cordial handshake. 'It seemed the only thing to do,' he said. But on succeeding visits, for he had still his studies to finish, he observed with some anxiety that his model's friendly attentions not only persisted but became progressively warmer and more intimate. The hesitating touch had now become a frank caress, and there was an expression in the creature's eye which could mean only one thing – Billy Orpen was loved by a monkey! Was he offended? Not a bit! He was but a youth and still a tyro in amatory experience, although subject no doubt, like most boys and girls, to the mysterious urgencies of sex. Besides, as he confessed, he had grown, if not yet to love, certainly to esteem his simian suitor, and if the latter could hardly be classed as a beauty by European standards, no more, for that matter, could he himself. The situation was difficult, but in the end common sense, with which he was well provided, prevailed. There could be no alliance. Popular prejudices were too strong; there was the Law to think of, too, and what about his career? He consulted the keeper, who, taking the only sensible course, arranged a swop, and his disconsolate charge, in exchange for a duck-billed platypus and a young South American peccary, was removed to another establishment. I will not attempt to describe the final scene, except to report that it was heart-breaking – and violent.

Back to Paris

PARIS, as I knew it when a young man, was a city of perpetual excitement. I explored it in wonderment and awe. The spectacle provided by its life and movement, its sounds and smells, never ceased to surprise me. I could never get accustomed to it, and even in rare intervals of exhaustion was always restored in time by some fresh and unexpected manifestation from without. I was the incurably naive provincial who could never hope to attain the easy self-sufficiency of those grave personages I marvelled at as they sat over a book with so formidable an air of detachment. In Paris we are never far from the Middle Ages. Villon may still be lurking round the corner, and to judge by popular physiognomy, Jehan Fouquet's descendants still survive in a land so often laid waste by war, pestilence, and famine. Our reveries, not un-attended by danger, may be interrupted by the Garde Républi-caine, which, passing like an antique cavalcade, quickens the blood and silences for a moment both the laughter and the murmurings of the people. 'Ca coûte cher, vous savez, mais c'est beau tout de même.' With such a remark the good bourgeois acknowledges the conflict which tears him for ever between avarice and a passion for grandeur.

A Night Out

In the company of Maurice Cremnitz, the *Prince des Poètes* (Paul Fort), and a young anarchist, I found myself in an obscure *bouge* near Les Halles one night. Our ideological friend, a handsome fellow, appeared distrait and in no mood for gaiety. Paul Fort, anxious to rouse him from this fit of melancholy, inquired, some-what tactlessly I thought, and in his habitual falsetto, what he had

43

been up to; were things not going well? 'Mais vous ne tuez pas, mon ami: surtout il faut tuer.' At this the young man began to show signs of nervous irritation, and to save him further discomfort and Paul Fort from possible reprisals, I proposed moving to another and a more respectable café on the Avenue d'Orléans, where Mme Fort was likely to be in wait for her wandering poet. Sure enough, we found her there in the sympathetic company of André Salmon, another member of our *cercle*, and the literary spokesman of *les Jeunes*. Paul Fort, having climbed on to his wife's lap, was good-naturedly nursed by her. This meeting-place was on my way home, too, and upon leaving the society, the Prince dismounting, accompanied me into the street. 'Où allez-vous?' he inquired. Perhaps he had another place of entertainment in view, but I answered somewhat mysteriously, 'Je retourne à la Montaigne.' The poet looked puzzled, for there are no mountains nor even hills in this district. Perhaps he suspected a hidden meaning in my playful allusion from *Also Sprach Zarathustra*.

At that time my family and I occupied a little house or *pavillon*, as it was called, in the Rue Dareau, beyond the Lion de Belfort. An almost mummified couple acting (though grudgingly) as concierges, inhabited a dark cell by the entrance. A studio in a little garden was at my disposal. In a word, it was ideal. We had made the acquaintance of a nice English doctor, who often visited us, less for medical reasons than in the hope of converting us to the doctrines of Auguste Comte of whom he was a fervent disciple. Unfortunately we were soon to seek his professional services.

A Birth and a Death

My wife had engaged a room in a private nursing home, for she was expecting a baby. When the time came the baby arrived in good order but alas such was not the case with the mother. In an establishment where, above all, a punctilious cleanliness might reasonably be counted on, she caught an infection. The French, so meticulous in most respects, in the matter of hygiene have sometimes incurred a suspicion of laxity.

It became necessary to move the patient to a hospital on the Boulevard Arago. This hospital was run by nuns and was spacious, airy and light, and I thought our prospects were brighter. I relied on Dr Tucker. A friend came to take charge of the children. But as the days passed there was no improvement; further complications ensued and a specialist was called in. My wife's mother arrived from England. She conferred with the specialist, whose fee for an operation was discussed and a bargain struck. The operation was performed but it was of no avail. After a few more days and nights the end came.

The usual column of smoke was rising from the tall chimney of the Crematorium of Père Lachaise. 'Ah, comme il fait chaud,' remarked the man with a shovel as, wiping his face, he collected a few calcined bones from the furnace.

I am not going to set down a catalogue of my sensations during this long-drawn-out crisis. Apart from my natural anxieties, I was oppressed by the futility of my visits, by my impotence and insignificance. Under the onslaught of high fever, my wife's mind fled to refuge in other places. In her own words, she was 'wandering in miraculous caves'. I could only beg for more opium. But there were moments of contact. 'I want some violets,' she said one morning. I hurried away at once: but where should I find violets? There were no shops near and there was no time to be lost. Descending the stairs, an open door gave a glimpse of an interior and, to my astonishment, there stood a table bearing a vase of violets! I crept in – the room was empty. Seizing the flowers, I returned in triumph. The violets were not quite fresh but they smelt of the good earth.

At the last vigil, a young nun sat by the bedside with me.

Silent and motionless in the dim light, she had the aspect of a Gothic carving. When next day, all was over, far from feeling cast down, I was seized by an incontrollable elation: I had had enough of despair. I rushed out on to the boulevard. The sun was shining gaily. I could have embraced any passer-by. I had escaped the dominion of death at last and was free. My friends were obviously mystified and no doubt shocked by my indecent behaviour, but I laughed at their long faces and called for wine.

But, needless to say, this state of exaltation was short-lived, and soon I relapsed into melancholy.

William McElroy and Others

I MET William McElroy in Chelsea at some studio party. A man of middle age and stature, of a comfortable girth, with grey hair just short of the venerable, and a voluble tongue, he was entertaining the company with jokes and funny anecdotes, to which a Belfast accent lent an extra piquancy. His evident good nature and general air of dubious prosperity, together with agreeable manners, recommended him to all. A kind of minor Horatio Bottomley, I thought. He got me to paint his portrait later and sat valiantly for several hours, though in the deepest gloom.

Oliver Gogarty and he were close friends. Though McElroy had the greatest reverence for intellect, he was unable himself to lay claim to much erudition. Nothing could silence him so effectually as a Latin quotation, and here of course Oliver was his master. They may have had business interests in common. McElroy, the coal merchant, could hardly be introduced into the circle of Gogarty's aristocratic buddies. Even Provost Mahaffy, who, though only (as far as I know) a scholar, was in the habit of prefacing his reminiscences with the words, 'As one of the most charming Emperors I ever met said to me ... ' could not very well be expected to greet a tradesman with enthusiasm.

But, to do him justice, McElroy's interests were not confined to coal. Starting his sporting career with wooden horses, he gradually worked up to real ones. He bought, for a song, a horse called Pastures New, got it trained, and entered it for the chief race on the Curragh, having put his bottom dollar on it and ten pounds for me. At the last moment, thinking the horse had caught a cold, he called off his bet, but the complete outsider won all the same. I think this was my first success on the Turf; the price was most favourable. McElroy, who had more than one iron in

47

the fire, soon recovered his buoyancy, and, not to be discouraged, acquired another horse, or rather part of a horse – the left hind leg, I think it was, which, in concert with the others, was doing very well. He and his fellow owners decided to run it for the Derby – the whole horse, I mean. McElroy kindly invited Dorelia and me to Epsom to see the race. A pub stands right alongside the paddock, and it was there we congregated. This pub, the only one on the course, was doing a roaring trade. It was swimming in beer. McElroy's horse was not successful on this occasion, but Dorelia, examining the list, picked a winner in another race simply because the animal's name appealed to her, so we had nothing to regret after all.

It was on this occasion that McElroy introduced me to Mr Sabini, the celebrated racecourse gangster.

Sabini

There was nothing gangsterish about Sabini's appearance or manner. Dressed correctly, without ostentation, he lacked only that extra touch of elegance proper to this occasion (a touch which I, too, had omitted); he spoke with that pleasing modesty and even diffidence we associate with a public school background. I understand that the cream of our criminal population derive from Eton, or at least claim to, but Sabini was singularly unpretentious. We took a stroll together. Seeing a group of Gypsies, I went up to them to exchange a few words of Romani speech. There is always a chance of picking up a variant of a word or a new locution. Sabini showed the greatest interest in this incident, and on leaving the Gypsies questioned me closely about these people. He was so used to seeing them at race meetings that he had just taken them for granted as part of the landscape, like jackdaws.

He then led me to the enclosure, which we entered without opposition, the mounted police on the course saluting my companion formally as we passed. Mr Sabini then bade me farewell, having some business to attend to. Soon after this event he retired, I believe, from public life, for I have heard nothing of him since. It is true he had rivals in his peculiar field of activity, and clashes did occur from time to time between the opposing organizations. I would be sorry to think such a nice man had got the worst of it, but the bookies might not agree with me here.

Sean O'Casey

It was through William McElroy that I made the acquaintance of Sean O'Casey. The two were close friends in spite of ideological differences. McElroy, in his role of capitalist, engaged the Court Theatre, Chelsea, for a season of O'Casey plays, with a cast of well-known actors and actresses from the Abbey Theatre, Dublin. These plays being a great success, O'Casey became a kind of hero of the hour. Elegant ladies emerging from the theatre would attempt to rush him as he, too, made his exit. But they got no encouragement from O'Casey. His questing nose was directed elsewhere, his myopic eyes held other images in view, his Dublin accent seemed to grow still thicker as, with caustic and perhaps too brief acknowledgments, and a cigarette behind his ear, he made his getaway. Had he not a beautiful Irish wife waiting for him? Or did she arrive later? I forget, but I don't forget her ...

McElroy, meanwhile, had undergone a kind of sea-change: the coal merchant had turned, as if by magic, into an impresario. As he descended the *escalier d'honneur* of the little Royal Court Theatre in his new evening clothes, complete with white tie and diamond studs, he looked as if he owned – well, Sloane Square including the pub next door.

I was taken down to a private room to meet my well-beloved friends, the delicious sisters Sally Allgood and Maire O'Neill, and others. There was nothing to drink but champagne; even the austere Sean had to have a glass. *His* intemperance is purely literary, and I used to think if he only drank more he'd blabber less. Pathos should be administered in drops, like medicine, never in a bucket; a subtle flavour rather than a thirst-quencher, to be guessed rather than gulped. Even sincerity itself is best taken for granted: it may be suspected but should never be displayed, for in itself it can be out of place, stupid and even indecent. Its only possible merit lies in the quality of thought in which it is en-wrapped.

However that may be, I could swallow any quantity of O'Casey's superb fun, and ask for more.

Thank you, great-hearted Sean!

*   *   *

Just as a too sustained attack on one's lachrymatory glands defeats itself, so does misapplied enthusiasm lead to discomfort. When McElroy, who had some experience in the boxing indus-try, felt my shoulders appreciatively and announced to a room-full of people my evident qualifications for a career in the Ring and his unalterable intention of bringing me out as a middle-weight, with the certainty of a championship to follow, I was not only incredulous but resentful. As he should have known, I had other ambitions which included no dependence on him.

Vaverteméskri Romané

IN OBSERVANCE of what was becoming a habit, i.e. an annual visit to Epsom Downs during Derby week, I became involved on one such occasion in an unusually complicated chapter of accidents.

I must say at once that these expeditions were in no way directly concerned with racing. I admired the horses certainly, but was out for other game. The reader will have remarked a predilection for a despised and outcast race, which I have betrayed before; and may have attributed this eccentricity to some weakness of the mind, or just a foolish pose.

I repudiate both these assumptions, though I might confess to a mysterious, though probably harmless, abnormality, the true significance of which I am unable to determine, but which is evidently deep-seated and persistent. I always went alone on these outings; indeed, in any circumstances, I prefer to visit the Gypsies unaccompanied, unless by a fellow initiate; but such are scarce and not always satisfactory. Imagine me then having a drink and a chat at one of the little open-air bars found near the racecourse in company with some members of an undistinguished tribe, whose name I have forgotten, but who included a young woman of remarkable charm, although a blonde. Struck by her almost classic style, I would have willingly sought her acquaintance (for I had my sketch-book) and no doubt would have done so, at least tentatively, but for the fact that she kept hovering at a distance, making communication difficult, except by means of the language of the eyes, in which she seemed to be very well versed.

My own responses were, I think, intelligible though guarded, for I was aware that among my companions there might be some of her brothers and possibly a husband ... These fellows, though not of the purest blood, might yet preserve some traces of an honourable if severe tradition derived from the more reputable of their assorted ancestors.

I ordered more beer, thinking to drown any such archaic prejudices and make it possible for me to convert a fellow-feeling, so far purely ocular, into a closer and more tangible reality; though how the necessary privacy was to be obtained amidst the hurly-burly of a racecourse I couldn't imagine. I would leave this detail to my vis-à-vis, who seemed untroubled by doubts of any sort and still smiled seraphically over her shoulder, while raising one hand as if pointing the way to a better land.

While thus preoccupied, my attention was diverted by unusual sounds which now made themselves heard close at hand; a kind of drumming accompanied by rhythmic chanting of a barbarous kind, the words being indistinguishable. It wasn't the Salvation Army, I felt sure, but what could it be then? Leaving my companions temporarily, I pushed my way through the crowd, to discover a band of wild outlandish people who were making their way slowly along while stopping here and there to pass the hat round. They were of both sexes, tall, dark, nonchalant and superb. Some beat on enormous tambourines, others led gigantic monkeys or rather apes, and all joined, when they felt like it, in the chant. Foreign Gypsies! or, as I have entitled this chapter, *Vaverteméskri Romané*.

Immensely excited by this encounter, I watched the fascinating spectacle, while considering what part of the world these people could have come from. The Balkans, no doubt, I decided: but there are many tribes in the Balkans, speaking variants of the Romani language in greater or less degrees of purity. I addressed one of the young men, using only such words as I thought would be understood in any dialect. '*Avés mansa, p'rala, te pias kitané.*' (Come, O Brother, with me that we may drink together.) The young man gazed into my eyes, but made no sign of comprehension. I tried again with no success. A young woman then joined us. From what she said in an unknown tongue, I caught the word Roumanian, or something like it. They understood *Roumanian*, she seemed to say, not *Romani* ...

These people, looking as if they had formed part of the hordes who at the beginning of the fifteenth century arrived in Vienna led by 'Dukes of Little Egypt' on horseback, disclaimed all knowledge of their language, their provenance and even their generic appellation. I was baffled. Were they deceiving me? As the band moved on I determined to pursue the matter further, but now an interruption occurred. I found myself wedged at the centre of a group of ill-favoured fellows, apparently engaged in a violent quarrel. Insults and even blows were being exchanged. As I attempted to extricate myself from this unpleasant situation, voices in the background reached my ears. '*Lurs skai, bâ, av avri!*' (Thieves here, friend, come away.) I had some sovereigns in my trouser pocket. Forcing my hand down, I found another hand already there! I seized and managed to withdraw it, and then with an herculean effort, freed myself to rejoin my Gypsy friends, who hurried me away, telling me I'd get *mârd* (kicked to death) if I stayed in the vicinity. But the leisurely approach of a policeman had now caused the racecourse gang to disperse.

This tale just shows how serviceable a slight acquaintance with the Romani tongue can be in a tight corner. I found I still had some coins left in my pocket, so after all 'more was lost on Mohae field'. My new friends practised a side-line in cozenage which was new to me. They had a roulette table which they set up in some advantageous spot with chaps posted in the offing to keep cave in case any inquisitive policemen appeared. When warned, the contraption was quickly disguised and removed to another quarter. It seemed a popular game.

Alas! I never saw the interesting blonde again and failed to overtake the foreigners, who seemed to have vanished as mysteriously as they came; yet on the whole, it was a good day's outing.

The mention of golden *sovereigns* in this narrative will roughly establish the date. It was pre-Bradbury, or as one might put it, B.B., but that is as near as I can get.

A Fisher King

EQUIHEN is a village of fisher-folk of a rather primitive sort. When I used to stay there the inhabitants were very poor (and still are); but there was one exception to the rule: this was a man of the name of Labouret. Labouret had been a fisherman, too, like the rest, but soon discovering in himself superior imagination, greater cunning and perhaps fewer scruples than his humbler colleagues, he quickly rose above them, not by catching more fish but by selling fishing tackle – and other commodities. He became a Man of Business, in fact. He started a shop, the only one in the village, which soon developed into a kind of emporium where everything necessary, and much that wasn't, could be obtained without making a journey into Boulogne (where you'd be diddled anyhow). The villagers felt that Labouret, being one of themselves, could almost be trusted; he, knowing them from A to Z, could trust them too, and did – up to a point. Whatever his system was, it worked, and before long he had most of his customers in his pocket.

When I looked him up a few years later, he was occupying the house I used to rent from him. I dare say he owned most of the village by that time. I asked after Mme Labouret, who was not present; I had greatly liked and admired this very fine and amiable old lady. Labouret without a word indicated a young woman at his side. This young woman certainly was pretty, but she looked very glum indeed and was speechless. Labouret himself was visibly ill at ease. In fact, the whole establishment seemed as if labouring under a curse. I made no further reference to the former Mme Labouret of course, although I would have been interested to know the circumstances of her death which I greatly regretted, but I left rather hurriedly without dropping any more bricks.

Euphemia at Boulogne

I WAS working along in my little studio at Equihen, when a knock at the door interrupted me. Opening the door I was confronted by a young man I had met in Paris. He was a Swedish poet who, I had been given to understand, lived and moved in a world of dreams. Entering, he explained the cause of his visit. Euphemia, an old friend of mine, was in Boulogne and very, very ill. I must come at once to see her.

'But I am not a doctor,' I protested. 'You must get a doctor.'

The young man was insistent. I must come at once, he repeated, in his slow Scandinavian way; Euphemia wished to see me.

Hoping this was only one of his dreams, I agreed to come, and we both walked into Boulogne together. I found Euphemia lying in bed.

'What's the matter?'

'Diphtheria,' she replied feebly.

'Open your mouth.'

I gazed into the cavern and seeing no trace of a white spot, told her to get up and dress at once, for we were going for a walk. She did so, and to my astonishment I now saw before me a charming boy in a sailor suit! It was in this costume that she had arrived from Paris. We went for our walk on the sands of Boulogne and in the evening, on my advice, Euphemia and the poet took a train back.

That dream was over.

Liverpool Revisited

UNDER the name of Francis Audrey I once broke a long sojourn in Paris to revisit Liverpool. Moved by a kind of nostalgia, or perhaps the magical *hiraeth* of my Welsh ancestry, I set out in the company of a young female whose appearance, I calculated, would go far to enhance my own: neither conforming strictly to the fashion of the day, but both sufficiently outlandish to ensure some degree of anonymity. As for the University College, where my disguise might betray instead of concealing my identity, I was to avoid that seat of learning, while allowing no consideration to prevent a renewal of my friendship with its Librarian, the Gypsy scholar John Sampson (or the *Rai*, to give Sampson his title).

Our meetings took place well outside the danger area of Brownlow Hill in various pubs known to us both of old; a favourite one being inconspicuously situated in a back street, near, but not too near, Sampson's home. The landlord of this establishment, known to us as *Hiifa Kekávi*, or Captain Kettle, was a man of the 'fancy' or *afficion*, and as such not entirely unversed in the Romani tongue. He responded with alacrity to the request for *dūi posh parno lils*,[1] at once producing two small glasses of a certain brand of whisky favoured by the Rai, my young companion contenting herself with a port and lemonade or some equally innocuous mixture, as the stronger drink was known to bring about immediate muscular reactions followed by collapse and even unconsciousness. Such a disaster was at all costs to be avoided, as much for reasons of convenience as of humanity. With what must have seemed to be the corpse of a young woman on our hands, we would hardly have reached our destination without comment from the public, or perhaps interference from

[1] Two small White Labels.

the police. Sampson and I agreed then in upholding the principles of temperance in the case of our fair companion, but the *posh parno lils* continued to repeat themselves with almost monotonous regularity. Why not order a few big ones, I thought, and have done with them till our next stop? But it was useless to hurry the Rai, who I knew was capable of remarkable obstinacy. This bald and inexorable scholar, under a haughty and sometimes overbearing exterior, nursed in secret the sensibility and the ardour of an adolescent. His innate romanticism, which had led him into such fruitful byways of literature and life, responded at once to the mildly clandestine conditions of these meetings. He enjoyed them, I think, and found in them a happy relief from the unwholesome constraints of his Library, with a chance to unbend temporarily while exchanging official responsibilities for the more open and genial mood proper to *Hüfa Kekávi*'s establishment.

A few more *posh parno lils*, and we took the air, our objective usually being a large piece of waste ground known as 'Cabbage Hall', though there was no Hall to be seen nor cabbages either, the site being occupied by the tents of our Gypsy friends only. A cab was needed, for we had some miles to go and night was already falling. The Rai marched ahead, for he knew the terrain. He made an imposing figure as he strode along, with his battered hat at a commanding angle, his cutty alight, his chin thrust out, and his powerful legs moving rhythmically. One could see that he was feeling good. A vehicle offering itself, we took our seats in it and were off on our adventures. The night I am thinking of was a dark one, but the darkness within our antiquated 'growler' was such as could positively be felt: this I realized when a distinct but not painful pressure applied locally to my person convinced me that someone had blundered. Addressing myself to the corner opposite our companion, where I judged the Librarian to be sitting, I remarked conversationally, 'By-the-by, Raia,[1] that's *my*

---

[1] Raia: voc. sing. of Rai, Sir.

leg you know.' This information was received in silence, but the pressure was instantly relaxed and it was in silence that we continued our journey. My interruption, though timely, had somehow intensified the surrounding gloom and I could see nothing ahead of us but a further series of *posh parno lils.*

The McNairs

THE McNairs taught what was known as *design* at our art school on Brownlow Hill, where I was supposed to teach *drawing*. In England alone, I believe, the functions of the two are held to be separate. In France the same word, *dessin*, includes both. This is only logical, for the two are complementary and should interlock, like the McNairs themselves, who always worked, as I imagine they played, in perfect unison.

Among the advance guard of *L'Art Nouveau*, a movement which originated in their home-town, Glasgow, and was destined to pervade Vienna, Germany and Paris, this cheerful couple saw themselves as Heralds of a New Age which was to sweep away the last remnants of Antiquity – not to speak of the Renaissance – to replace them, along with their decrepit human survivors, by a new and infinitely more vigorous manifestation of creative energy, liberated at last from the servitude of tradition, and still more drastically from the tyranny of nature itself.

Warming as such a programme was bound to be to one as young and naive as myself, I suffered a distinct lowering of temperature upon being confronted with the works of the two charming protagonists. I responded as frigidly to the curly door-knockers and the rectangular tin troughs fitted with night-lights, etc., of the one, as to the quaintly pretty embroideries of the other, in which bulbous gnomes or fairies figured largely in surroundings of a totally unidentifiable order. To me they might have been the dreams of a babe, signifying nothing, or at least nothing I knew anything about. When pressed by McNair for a personal appraisal of his industry, I with much reluctance complying, the honest fellow, forgetting that he had volunteered a similar estimate of my own efforts, broke down, saying he would just like to swim and swim right out to sea till he drowned. Without going to these lengths he did leave Liverpool eventually to return to his native land, where, I was told, forswearing Art, he became a first-class postman.

His brother-in-law MacKintosh, whose friendship I enjoyed in Chelsea, was of course a much more serious figure: an architect of indisputable distinction, he certainly left his mark on the face of things to come. *L'Art Nouveau*, after a short period of hectic commercialization, became an object of ridicule, to be followed by the more important innovations of Surrealism, Fauvism, Cubism and other experiments of our times.

In Search of Charley Boswell

HARKING back to earlier days, I have told how I made the acquaintance of Esmeralda Groome, née Boswell, when she was camping on the Wirral, and later met her younger and equally eccentric sister Dorelia, who shared a van with, I am sorry to say, a red-haired Irish tinker. In spite of this mésalliance, Dorelia Boswell was in other respects a splendid specimen of her race. She left a deep and permanent impression of beauty and child-like candour on my wax-like mentality.

I had heard of another prominent member of the family, Charley Boswell, otherwise known as Charley Lock, or *Klizn* in the Romani tongue. He was well spoken of, so upon visiting North Wales on one occasion I got wind of this Gypsy's presence in the neighbourhood, and determined to track him down. I was at this time at Bangor, having just returned from Beaumaris where I had pursued and run to earth a young female belonging to the Clan of Abram Wood, whom I found working in the chief hotel of the town, and disguised, to my embarrassment, in the uniform of a menial. My efforts to persuade the young recreant to reform her ways, shed this livery of servitude and return to the open road, were unavailing, so, leaving her conversion for another day, I set out to find Charley Boswell. According to the *patrin* or secret indications of the fraternity, one was most likely to find him near a certain village a few miles from Menai.

The day was magnificent. Although blazing hot, the air was light and heady like champagne. I strode along at a great pace, and, with a little extra length of leg, could have done justice, I felt, to a pair of seven league boots, though I hadn't so far to go. Passing through Menai, I noted (and avoided) the proximity of the police station. Little did I dream that I was to visit this sinister establishment ere long and of my own volition. Upon reaching the village I aimed at, my observations led me about a mile further where I found an encampment of several ornate vans and Charley Boswell himself with his family. Having introduced myself, I was made welcome, accommodated with a chair, and, it being tea-time, the beverage known to the Gypsies by the poetic title of *mūterimangori* was served in excellent style. Charley, who was noted for his good manners and charm of personality, was geniality itself, and moreover he and his family, I was glad to see, shared and were to perpetuate, no doubt, the good looks of this branch of the Boswell tribe. They spoke a good and partly inflected dialect of Romani, though it was far from having the depth and complexity of that of the tri-lingual descendants of Abram Wood, known as the *Kalé* or dark people.

Time passed in agreeable gossip and discussion on 'affairs of Egypt', for we had a number of friends and acquaintances in common. As I rose to leave, Charley apologized for his apparent inhospitality, assuring me that were it not for the fact that his wife was abed in expectance of a new baby at any moment, he could have afforded me shelter and rest for the night in one of the vans. Before I left, however, he made me promise to call again next day, for he was sure I could find a night's lodging near by.

I felt no desire for sleep, and upon inquiry was not distressed in the least to find no bed available in the village. The evening was of a warmth and mellowness unusual even in this zone, where nature contrives to disseminate and hold longer than elsewhere the reflection of a sun already hidden beneath the ocean's rim. Subdued by the sweet solemnity of the scene, I realized I stood in truth on holy ground: for was not this the sacred island to the Great Lord of the Sea, the Celtic Poseidon: was it not Inys Mon?

But at this point my musings were interrupted by the approach of two figures, one of whom presented the unmistakable silhouette of a policeman. Without greeting or ceremony this helmeted busybody proceeded to seek an explanation of my appearance in the district. He inquired my name and business for a start. I gave my name but confessed to have no business. 'Have you no lodging?' 'I was unable to find any in the village but am quite content to sleep out on so warm a night, in fact I prefer to do so.' 'Have you no money?' 'I have sufficient for my needs at present, thank you.' 'Have you proofs of your identity?' 'Yes, I think so.' I searched in my pocket and brought out a letter written in the 'deepest' Romani from John Sampson, Librarian of University College, Liverpool. This letter in no way reassured the policeman, who, having studied it for some moments, handed it back, remarking, 'This looks very suspicious.' 'Yes,' said his companion, who had been looking over his shoulder and read the address, 'they do say there's some very funny people comes from the University.'

In spite of his suspicions, the policeman now said he thought his wife might let me have a bed if I was prepared to pay for it, mentioning a substantial sum. I declined this offer, saying I would be quite happy if they would kindly leave me alone. 'But you are breaking the Law.' 'Perhaps, but I am breaking nothing else,' I replied and was moving away when one of my interlocutors called out, 'You could try the Castle. The Marquis of Anglesey's got a Pantomime on, and he'd be sure to let you in.' Whether this was meant as a gibe or not I cannot decide, but I thought I would in fact try the Castle. Anything for a change of company! The Castle was near at hand. On my ringing the bell, the butler came out. He was quite the nicest of butlers. On hearing my predicament, he seemed deeply touched, but had to confess he hadn't a single spare bed to dispose of – people were even sleeping on the billiard-tables! He was full of apologies, and I left feeling by no means cast down but on the contrary rather elated, as one who has made a new friend.

The problem facing me now was how to avoid the custodian

1

Augustus John

of the Law, or *Prastermengro*,[1] who, with his hired assistant or *muscro*,[2] were still lurking on the main road as I returned. They were not going to lose sight of me; that was certain. A plan formed in my mind which would not only inconvenience my persecutors but baffle them and at the same time ensure my keeping the appointment with Charley Lock next day. Turning my back on the village I walked briskly towards Menai. From time to time I paused to make sure of being followed. Upon arriving I found the police station I had noticed in the morning, and, stopping, rang the bell. After a short wait the door was opened by a policeman who was evidently none too pleased at being roused from his slumbers. I said I wished to lodge a complaint of interference from a constable in the village of —— The policeman, having noted this down in a book, eyed me narrowly. Then, having made up his mind, he advised me to cross the Menai Bridge; once on the other side, he said, I would be outside his jurisdiction and might do as I thought fit. With that we parted. I crossed the bridge and, in full view of the helmeted figure and his companion who had conscientiously followed me thus far, threw myself under a hedge and slept. Next morning I walked into Bangor where I hired a trap and returned for another pleasant séance with the Gypsies. As I was driven through the village, I passed my two ill-favoured ones, who gazed at me with astonishment, but I made no sign of recognition. I fail to remember the name of this village but it was not the one ending in Llandisiliogogogoch.

---

[1] *Prastermengro*, from *praster*, to run: one who runs you in.

[2] *Muscro*, a Gypsy word; originally *mūiescro*, pertaining to the mouth: a hue-and-cry man.

Move on! A Glance at the Gypsies

JOHN BUNYAN the Tinker, or as some say the Gypsy (metal-work is an old Gypsy craft), for he describes himself, if I remember rightly, as belonging to an 'outlandish and despised people', spent a good deal of his time in gaol for airing religious views then unpopular with the authorities. Being literate, he was able to occupy his enforced leisure in writing the immortal works we so much admire today.

Ordinary Gypsies cannot for the most part read or write, and, nomads by tradition and upbringing, are accustomed to gain a living while moving about the country with their horses, tents and wagons. Devoted to this way of life, they are more likely to find the discipline of imprisonment both irksome and unrewarding (to put it mildly) than other people; but their petty misdemeanours hardly call for great severity. Criminality is rare among them.

For some years, however, a new drive against the Gypsies has been in operation in the southern and some other counties of England, with the aim, apparently, of exterminating 'these anti-social pests', as they were described in Nazi Germany. Although this policy may not include the summary methods of Himmler – the 'hedge-crawlers' (to use another Nazi epithet) are not caught and gassed outright as if they were Jews – the treatment adopted will prove no less lethal in the long run. Harried into the slums of our big towns or the 'ground-worm' infested filth of New Forest concentration camps, they are condemned to squalor, disease and degradation. Freedom being their one and only political concept, these born conservatives are strangers to the ballot box (but not to the recruiting officer), and are thus overlooked by the Welfare State. If some of the ones who are better off are persuaded to make use of 'council houses', such recreants have been known, disconcertingly, to repay conversion by setting up their tents in the garden while according the amenities of the house to their animals.

Francis Hides Groome, who was an eminent Gypsy scholar of a past generation, wrote in the *Encyclopaedia Britannica*:

> The better sort of Gipsies are quick witted, courteous, likeable and trustworthy when trusted. Untrammelled by prejudices and vexed by no lofty ambition, they have picked up a sort of peripatetic philosophy, lead a pleasant cuckoo-like existence and make the best of life ...
>
> Great criminals are few among them ...
>
> The best gipsy is the gipsy *au naturel*, the life-long dweller in country lanes; and he like all *ferae naturae* is threatened with extinction. Gipsies' virtues are largely their own, an outcome of open-air life; their vices are ascribable to centuries of oppression, which has left them a singular compound of deep-seated gloom and quick-silver light-heartedness, and has made them suspicious and hostile towards the rest of mankind.

One may add that the last-mentioned attitude is fully reciprocated by the majority referred to, though without similar warrant. Having quoted an excellent, though no longer quite contemporary authority, I now add a letter which I have recently received from a living Gypsy:

Dear Sir,

As a caravan dweller I read in to-day's News Chronicle with much interest and pleased to think someone has a feeling for Romany and his cattle. I for one no what it is to be moved on. Ordenary Folk grumble at next to nothing. But had they to put up with the life of a Gipsy Im sure they would think

again. Ive no need to tell you what a Gipsy and his horse has
to go through, you must already know. Some Folk may say
why does he have to put up with it. Why dont they come off
the Road and live in houses and work in a factory. Well it
would be like taking a wild Bird and putting it in a cage.

E. E. SMITH
Caravan, Little Brookham, Surrey.

If asked what it is that has fascinated some people about Gypsies
(a fascination which is incurable), I might allude to their physical
comeliness; their pleasant manners; their fastidiousness; their
ready wit and gaiety combined with pride; their essential honesty
even when combined with prevarication; their love of children;
and their exotic language and strange taboos – all these I might
mention and still leave unexplained a mysterious something of
which I do not know the name, but which I recognize with a
thrill from a mile off.

But wandering Gypsies (though always wandering with a
purpose) are not everybody's fancy. The grocers of Kent have
now adopted the precaution of pasting up the notice over their
shops, 'No Gypsies served here'. This sweeping and discriminatory
generalization, coming from a class of uncreative middlemen
popularly known for their practice of mixing sand with the sugar
(on the Continent, the designation *épicier* is but rarely understood
as a compliment), moved me lately to send a letter of protest to
The Times, resulting in a flood of highly sympathetic expressions
of opinion from friends of the Gypsies all over the country, with
only one dissident, a correspondent whose communication was
both abusive and anonymous.

Without the testimony of Gypsy scholars the world over, these
letters prove that among ordinary people there are not a few who
have found themselves well repaid by friendly contact with the
dark strangers in our midst, once the attitude of suspicion and

hostility, induced by ages of ignorant persecution, has been replaced by the bonhomie and merriment more natural to them, as to other children. For Gypsies never quite grow up. They remain naïf and transparent even in their humbug and should have no difficulty in entering, when the time comes, into that Kingdom promised by another Wanderer, who like them was not exactly *persona grata* with the Authorities, nor, one may add, with Big Business, in Kent or anywhere else. Long before the age of myxomatosis, the Gypsies (and others) did their share in reducing our superfluity of rabbits, though at some risk; and one wonders by what means they have replaced this popular and important item in the poor man's larder. Hedgehogs, I know, are only at their best in the autumn, and the Gypsy is a fastidious eater. Doubtless the grey squirrel will to some extent fill the gap, being a proven delicacy, with, in addition, a bonus attached to every tail, but if the worst comes to the worst, there is always the *Bare Hochipen* or Big Trick to fall back upon. Credulity at any rate is inexhaustible, thank goodness.

Those of us who love liberty and enjoy variety must surely stand up for a small and politically powerless people from the East, who have made this country their own and have enlivened and ornamented our country-side since the fifteenth century while, for the most part, preserving their racial integrity, their traditional customs, and even in parts their ancient language, in a usually hostile world. However, it is a world they love and flourish in, if left to their own way of life (which by the bye is now imitated by hosts of highly respectable holiday-makers, so there must be something in it). In any case, before condemning these people out of hand, it would be as well to make their acquaintance. This may take some time and trouble, but with goodwill and good manners, it may be worth while and even rewarding for such as have a taste for human nature, and no axe to grind.

Early Indiscretions

I USED to be rather shy and undemonstrative as a schoolboy, except when on the football field, where I displayed considerable dash. Out on the sands for official exercise, too, I was capable of remarkable initiative which could sometimes be embarrassing, as when, without a by-your-leave, I would strip and, seemingly 'possessed', perform miracles of speed and agility, to the astonishment of all, and especially the Head, who would stop and contemplate my complicated evolutions with an expression which seemed to betray the painful irresolution of Authority confronted by the Ungovernable. Perhaps these performances awakened in the schoolmaster's mind long-suppressed feelings dating from a classical background, and induced in him a kind of moral paralysis, for I was never punished for these departures from the academic rule, though I remained under the suspicion incurred, upon the discovery by the Head's brother, when he was second-in-command, of certain studies of the nude which I would have preferred to keep to myself, but which the ex-policeman hurriedly requisitioned, no doubt to enrich his private collection, for I heard no more of them.

But not all my early strivings were misunderstood. A portrait of the Devil turned out successfully. It was a good likeness, I thought, and so did Father Bull, who should know; he said that under the Mask of Evil I had succeeded in disclosing something of the beauty of a Fallen Angel.

Father Bull, at this time employed as tutor to a few pupils, was a young man with whom I became friendly. He often joined me and the other boys at our favourite bathing place, known as The Point, on the north shore of Tenby, and at a sufficient distance from the town to permit of perfect freedom or even, as some

70

might object, licence. From this little promontory one could dive straight into deep water, and it was here I was taught to swim by the simple process of being thrown into it.

My Catholic friend, who used to draw a bit himself, encouraged me in the practice. He seemed to see some merit, or at least promise, in my sketches, although being a stickler for purity (in Art), he found my nude studies sometimes faulty, in that they were not always nude *enough* for his taste. A thorough classicist, any concessions to modern notions of propriety were, in his view, *improper*. When I asked him to explain certain anatomical anomalies to be found in the traditional treatment of the female figure, which had begun to puzzle me, he was unable, or unwilling, to throw any light on the subject, nor, I may add, has anybody else done so to this day. This matter seems to me important, and I think of seeking Arthur Koestler's help in my perplexity, for he seems to know everything, and it is too late to consult Freud himself, who indeed, for all I know, may have treated the subject already, but, considering its delicacy, probably in Latin, a language which, although taught at school, I have never thoroughly mastered.

Lunching in style

When Cardinal Vaughan visited Tenby to officiate at the dedication of the new church of St Teilo, Father Bull, with whom the Cardinal was staying, was kind enough to invite me, among a few others, to luncheon. Unused to such social conditions, and overawed by the grandeur of the principal guest, who looked every inch a Prince of the Church, I was surprised by the general levity of the conversation during the course of the meal. Everybody but I seemed to be enjoying himself, especially the Cardinal. Father Bull, too, was in the best of spirits, and naturally, for the occasion marked the crowning of his labours in the successful establishment of this new outpost of his faith and he had collared the Cardinal! The church was built and sanctified: was it not pardonable to relax for a little while and indulge that spirit of laughter and fun, which, first discovered in childhood, should never be wholly abjured? We cannot all be blessed saints, and for that reason the lesser joys of poor humanity are not to be frowned at. Remembering Cana, Father Bull sent the port round again. Without being able to follow all the witty sallies which now excited general hilarity, some of them I thought were not, in substance, unlike those I was accustomed to at our bathing parties at Lydstep and other out-of-the-way places. In these circumstances I was quite capable of enjoying much without turning a hair; but here, strange to relate, it only resulted in embarrassing me, while my complexion deepened from bright pink to a deep crimson. At a given moment Father Bull, noticing this phenomenon and unable to master an increasing tendency to facetiousness, inquired pointedly if I *painted*. This brought the house down, and with all eyes directed at me, I wished myself safely under it. Even now, such a question would induce a discomfort and cause a slight blush to modify for a little while my customary pallor.

The Hermaphrodite

In my own experience, I have found the nearest living approach to the Greek ideal in the person of a hermaphrodite seen in Paris some years ago, to which monstrosity I was introduced by a friend with a passion for the bizarre.

Displayed stark naked on a couch, it possessed all the attributes and some of the charm of a woman save for one notable absence, here, as in a masterpiece by Phidias, glossed over and left blank; except for the surprising introduction of a feature borrowed from the other sex, which rudely raised its head in defiance of all probability as well as of artistic convention, though, incidentally, in a somewhat abbreviated form.

Unable to control my curiosity, and forgetting my manners, I boldly inquired in my own French: 'Pardon, Madame, ou Monsieur, quand il vous arrive de sentir le besoin de l'amour, comment faites-vous?' 'Mais, Monsieur, je me masturbe,' was the answer, delivered without hesitation, to my naive and really inexcusable impertinence ...

At Galway

WHEN staying in Galway, I made a few contacts with local society, but came after a while to recognize some of the more redundant elements of the population I used to meet with while strolling about the town. These types seemed, like myself no doubt, to have nothing better to do than to 'pass the time', but were animated, I couldn't help thinking, by very different motives. Natives of the town or district could hardly be expected to view the life and movement around them with a stranger's curiosity and wonder. Long familiarity had blurred for them the peculiar rhythm of the place, a rhythm of which, probably, they had never been really aware, unless subconsciously, as children – and which was, in any case, already well on the way to extinction under the deadly blight of commerce and the blundering exigences of law.

The shawled women murmuring together on the quays, with the white complex of the Claddagh glimmering across the harbour; the echoing streets; the purple waters of the bay under a weeping sky – all such phenomena were taken for granted, and I was experienced enough to keep my observations of them strictly to myself, if I should happen to strike up acquaintance with a fellow time-waster in one of the innumerable bars with which this sea port is provided. For I felt that if I was indeed 'passing the time', I was none the less engaged in storing my mind with impressions which, I promised myself, would one day be realized not only to my own private satisfaction but to the edification of the world at large. This thought sustained me, while my fellow pilgrims, instead of looking outside, as I did, for encouragement, were apt to seek within for a quicker antidote to boredom and a more effectual means of exorcising, if only for a while, the grinning spectre of futility.

Timon of Athens

I once found myself in the company of some interesting fellows, with whom I was invited to sit down and take a drink. One of them, whom I took to be the leader because he paid the rounds, remained with me after the others had left. This young man was not in the best of spirits; he was disillusioned, it seemed. He had put his faith in others and had been deceived. Always generous (for he was well off), he had been surrounded with flatterers, who, under the guise of friendship, consumed his drinks and his cigarettes ('threepence a packet'), only to ridicule him behind his back. Such, said the melancholy youth, had been his experience of humanity. 'I am like Timon of Athens,' he said. He repeated sadly, 'Timon of Athens, that's me!'

Another social event took place at the Railway Hotel, in a private room, such as were provided here before the hotel was modernized and lost its character. This was more than a friendly meeting; it developed into something like an International Test Match, but minus any pretence of fair play. The teams consisted of about six young men on the Home side and just myself on the visitors'. The question to be decided was: which would be under the table first? Well, to make a long story short, I found myself in the end, alone and upright. Stepping carefully over the recumbent forms of my opponents, I left the building, and having nothing particular to do, walked down to Flaherty's Bar on the New Dock to have a drink and a chat with the barmaid, a girl I admired greatly. Her name, Kitty McGee, describes her perfectly, though she had something more oblique and veiled in her look than her name denoted.

I would not have told this story if I had any intention of

revisiting Galway City, but since the Claddagh has been demolished and replaced by the concrete tenements of the Republic, the classic shawls exchanged for cheap finery from Manchester, and Kitty married, it will be better, safer and more rewarding to try another port in future.

Gordon Craig

IT MIGHT have been at Will Rothenstein's that I first made Gordon Craig's acquaintance. Afterwards I used to meet him in a side bar of The Markham, a pub in the King's Road, Chelsea, where one could lunch. He was often found there in the company of Martin Shaw, a musician who shared his taste for folk-song but in a more professional way.

At that time Craig was addicted to Walt Whitman, and besides had recently come to acknowledge the spiritual authority of Tolstoi. *War and Peace* was for him a sacred text, and the Christian Anarchist Count was accepted as the herald and expositor of a better world.

As for Whitman, I, too, had been aroused by the barbaric yawp, though much earlier. The gentle Jesus used to make me cry as a child, but since adolescence it is Walt who alone similarly affects my lachrymal glands (especially when he is read aloud by Orson Welles). Making no pretensions to divinity, he has super-seded the Greco-Jewish Man-God, with whom, in other respects and from a different angle, he has much in common.

Craig, exquisitely adjusted to his Craiginess, might sometimes be considered a little pernickety. The appearance of a dancer with oriental leanings, Ruth St Denis, had greatly attracted me, but Gordon Craig did not approve of her. There was something *sinister* about her, he said, though he did not dispute her accomplishment. I was undeterred by this and wrote to her, craving a sitting, but my request was disregarded.

As is well known, Craig was all against the modern theatre, with its imitation realism and actor worship. 'Why,' I once ventured to ask, 'do you not get a circus-tent, travel the country and give your "representations" freely in your own way?' 'But

I don't know how to make a tent,' he replied. This I thought rather pedantic, but I see his point. To quote John Sampson, who quoted Walter Raleigh in another context, he was apt to be 'as jealous of his privileges as a maiden aunt at a Dorcas meeting'.

Later on Craig acquired the Arena Goldoni, in Florence, and set up a school of the Theatre. He collected but few pupils, but these were taught to fence. Meanwhile, he carried on his journal, *The Mask*, which he wrote mostly himself. Anyone interested in the Commedia dell' Arte had better get hold of numbers of *The Mask*. I went to see his production of Ibsen's *Vikings* in London. For 'scenery' he employed simple cubes of various heights. When motoring in Provence a year or two ago, we discovered a wonderful hill-town in the mountains behind Nice. As we approached, the town presented a frontage of tall cube-like habitations rising from the precipitous rock. I was instantly reminded of Craig's designs.

Having explored the dark and narrow alleys of the ancient town I returned to the central *place* where I found a game in progress. It was a form of basket-ball, played by young people of both sexes, who for the occasion were attired in garments of a remarkable economy: but there was no evidence of false modesty and certainly no exhibition of old-fashioned coquetry to be noted. I was watching young France disporting itself in a medieval ambience.

Having dined at a restaurant on the outskirts of the town, we were about to leave when some new clients arrived. These consisted of a romantic-looking but elderly gentleman in a black cloak and a sombrero, accompanied by some ladies. This was Gordon Craig. It seems he lived there!

Heroically uncompromising as an Artist, as Craig has always been, he has lately made one concession to our vulgar age. His broadcasts have surely been among the best ever delivered.

Gwendolen John

MY SISTER'S preference for slums and underground cellars never quite won my approval. I am attracted by both, but not as a potential resident. The robust paganism of my outlook, intensified by the fact of consanguinity, resulted in a conflict in which fraternal jealousy was too often unable to repress its instinctive movements of impatience with what seemed to me a renegade and injurious philosophy, diametrically opposed to the system, perhaps more muscular than intellectual, which I then professed.

When soon after leaving the Slade she installed herself in a kind of dungeon near Fitzroy Street, into which no ray of sunlight could ever penetrate, I openly demurred. It was cheap, but was it truly economical? Would not her health suffer in this gloomy vault? Was the lighting, what there was of it, suitable for painting? It is true the ordinary studio, with its glaring top-light, is usually an unpleasant place, but this, I thought, was going too far. But no, Gwen was delighted with her new quarters and would not listen to my arguments. She never did. The same indifference to physical considerations characterized her throughout her life. The apartment at Meudon which she occupied for so many years was certainly not subterranean, being about six storeys above ground, but it was inconvenient and situated in no enviable quarter; and later on, when she moved to Rue Babie, her new residence consisted of a mere shed, hardly weatherproof, erected in half an acre of waste ground. My objections to this policy of self-neglect, entirely motivated by my regard for her well-being, were met with ridicule. I was only betraying an absence of sensibility and a fundamentally 'bourgeois' state of mind. Besides she had her cats to consider. They came first. It was these animals which prevented her coming to England on account of quarantine regulations, and

79

their necessities which made an occasional visit to her father in Wales a matter of insuperable difficulty. Though she had acquired a cottage in Hampshire, after one short sojourn she never returned to it.

With some talented student friends she passed some time in Paris under the tutelage of Whistler. It was thus she arrived at that careful methodicity, selective taste and subtlety of tone which she never abandoned. Though she owed much to this training, her power of drawing was entirely original as was her more than aesthetic sense of life. Her friendship with Rodin played an important part in her career. He recognized her gifts and acclaimed her as 'a fine artist'. It is not generally known that the statue commemorating Whistler which Rodin was commissioned to execute for this country, was modelled after my sister. This magnificent work, of which one arm is incomplete, takes the shape of a colossal female figure, slightly draped and holding a medallion with the Artist's portrait thereon. It was not approved by the Committee, who decided to acquire a replica of the 'Bourgeois de Calais' instead.

Gwen, though she became so much of a recluse, was by nature by no means lacking in *joie de vivre*. Her eye for character and her native humour enabled her to appreciate the gay as well as the tragic aspects of the *Comédie Humaine*.

Of an extreme timidity in a social sense, she was always capable of demonstrating a dauntless courage and a formidable strength of will. Her pride, honesty and devotion to what she took to be her duty, combined, under the compulsion of a sufficient motive, to transform her into an irresistible force. This gentle soul was then adamant in resolution and would stick at nothing. Having embraced the Catholic faith she became, it might be said, more pious than the Pope. My Jesuit son, Elphin, used sometimes to attempt the conversion of his father and once, when he was arguing that I had nothing to lose but everything to gain by

3 : 4
5 : 6

accepting the true Religion, Gwen happened to enter the room and, overhearing this line of reasoning, instantly corrected the ardent young casuist. 'You are quite wrong,' she said. 'One accepts the Truth because it is the Truth, and not for any advantage; indeed, for the love of God one is prepared to lose everything, even life; as if that mattered!' The cold contempt of these words impressed me while it silenced my son ...

In her later period my sister painted numerous portraits of nuns; she also left some landscapes, done chiefly in Brittany, besides many drawings of children, women, flowers and cats. Her coloured drawings are often repeated dozens of times, with slight variations. Few on meeting this retiring person in black, with her tiny hands and feet, a soft, almost inaudible voice, and delicate Pembrokeshire accent, would have guessed that here was the greatest woman artist of her age, or, as I think, of any other.

The end came when, feeling the need of a change of air, Gwen John took the train to Dieppe. She collapsed on arriving. She had brought no baggage whatever, but as it turned out had not forgotten to make in her will a suitable provision for the cats ...

F

Isadora Duncan

I HAD never seen Isadora Duncan dance when I met her first, but I had heard her praises sung by people of discrimination, and it was with much curiosity and even excitement that, by a lucky chance, I made her acquaintance.

But was I to be disappointed? I tried to adopt a prudent reserve, for I had been 'had' before ...

The appearance in England, some years earlier, of the dancer Maud Allan, had been followed by regrettable excesses, reminding one of the less creditable phenomena of religious conversion. The Prime Minister of the time was said to have caught the epidemic, which, it seems, first made its appearance in the upper levels of society. It was William Orpen, by then pretty well established on the fringe of fashion, who brought me the glad tidings. The credulous little Dubliner, his eyes moister than usual, assured me that the new dancer was something unheard of. Not only was she possessed of the secret of levitation, but, I was assured, she was able to ripple her bones as though they were made of india-rubber! Without questioning the advantages of the latter accomplishment, and to change the subject, which was beginning to bore me, I promised to look in at the theatre and examine this prodigy for myself. And so one evening I found myself standing at the back of the dress circle awaiting my conversion, but without much confidence.

The performance started with a dance illustrative of Mendelssohn's 'Spring Song'. I retained imperfect memories of my fathers' rather laborious renderings of this and other works by a composer to whom, as a good Victorian, he was much addicted. Miss Allan's interpretation could not be called laboured; it was extremely brisk: there was much rippling of the arms (but not the legs), and the performer's other movements seemed to be equally unnecessary and repetitive.

My response was violent, and would have been audible but for the storm of applause which drowned it.

I had had enough, and was turning to go when a messenger approached me with an invitation from the management to come 'behind' and join a selection of other enthusiasts in doing homage to the exquisite terpsichorean. I declined the offer and hastily left the building.

So, thought I, such was the classical dance as conceived in the U.S.A.

But I was wrong. Isadora Duncan also hailed from the Wild West.

*   *   *

I had been lunching with the Princess Murat at the Ritz in Paris. On leaving the hotel we found Isadora waiting at the entrance. She was accompanied by a tall, handsome personage. It was Walter Rummel, whom later I was to know as 'the Archangel'. My companion, who 'knew everybody', presented me, and a few words were exchanged before their car took them away.

I was left with the impression of having met a remarkable and highly sympathetic personality. The dancer's countenance, which was round and open, breathed candour and gaiety, and her figure, although veiled disturbingly in some shadowy and to me un-identifiable material, disclosed the accents and contours of an unfashionable opulence, but betraying at no point any trace of fatigue or the over-blown. Tall rather than short, her proportions would, I think, upon analysis, have fulfilled satisfactorily all the requirements of the antique *Section d'Or*, and her costume *à la mode* showed the imprint of a master couturier. Raymond Duncan would not have approved of his sister's attire; but then he dis-approved of her habits in general. These cocktails, these smart restaurants, these fashionable togs; how wrong it all was! How expensive, how deleterious, and – yes – how vulgar!

I often stopped to gaze through the window of Raymond's establishment in the Rue de Seine. Within, a faithful little band bent over their looms as they wove the woollen fabrics from which were made the simple garments prescribed by the Master, and affected by him as by all the members of his cult. This garment or *chiton* is worn by both sexes and may be long or short. With a pair of sandals, it suffices both for warmth and decency; it is becoming and dignified; it is also cheap and durable, compared to the evanescent products of fashion and commerce. It may be unsuitable for the business man, for it seems to have no pockets, but a bag may be carried over the shoulder at the end of a stick. A top hat, unless a very old and obsolete one, would certainly be out of place, and as for general wear, it will be long, I think, before the *chiton* comes into fashion – though it might well prove popular at the seaside.

After this meeting I saw nothing more of Isadora till she came to London on a professional visit. I was among those who welcomed her.

Since she had been wondering where would be the best place to stay, I had suggested the Cavendish Hotel in Jermyn Street, which I knew to be extremely well appointed; besides, its proprietress, my old and esteemed friend Mrs Rosa Lewis, constituted in herself, I should say, a sufficient 'draw' for anybody. Americans, I knew, took to Rosa Lewis on sight, and acclaimed her as the archetype of an age and way of life of which she appears to be the only representative still to be met with. Unique in England, she has become a legend in the States. We shall certainly never see her like again, though when I come to think of it, her spiritual ancestry being Elizabethan or even Chaucerian, the immortal strain is bound to reappear in the future, even if it is, for reasons of state, carefully disguised.

My suggestion was acted upon. Isadora, however, took little advantage of the talents and charm of her hostess, or the unusual amenities of the house, and kept to her own quarters, but only for a few days. I have often found that my enthusiasms only excite incredulity and suspicion in others, and I cannot claim to have made, in my time, a single convert to any cause dear to me. Perhaps, though but a few yards from Piccadilly Circus, once considered to be the hub of our Empire, and its spiritual navel, dominated as it is by the soaring image of the god of love, Jermyn Street, would not at once strike the foreigner as the distinguished thoroughfare it has some claim to be. It will have for him, no doubt, the air of a secondary or even a back street, but back streets sometimes fill front pages, especially in London, and Isadora, uninstructed, was unaware of this as of the many other incongruities of our capital. At the zenith of her short career her outlook had been conditioned by the more stately background of her continental triumphs, and, childlike, she judged this to be indispensable, or at least appropriate. Was she then exclusively committed to the expensive mediocrity of the smart hotel? The answer is no. But in this case she soon abandoned the Cavendish and moved to the Berkeley, or perhaps some other home from home – I have forgotten. Here, at any rate, her visibility would be increased; there was her box-office to be considered ... I continued to visit her, of course, though I sometimes missed the peculiar cachet of Mrs Lewis's establishment; a cachet which might escape the casual visitor, and which Isadora, isolated in her private apartment, remained unaware of.

After supper the Archangel would usually seat himself at the piano, and Isadora, from time to time, as the spirit moved her, rose and danced. She wore a loose short-sleeved gown, pleated, of terra-cotta silk. Raising her arms heavenwards, and her now transfigured face too, she would take a step or two forward, sideways, backward, forward ... and that was all! But the dancer moved as if at the behest of unseen powers and she moved in rapture, not abasement …

Isadora had complained rather bitterly of the scarcity of millionaires in this country. Elsewhere she had been accustomed to keep one or two within call, upon whom to discharge the burden of such practical matters as she was constitutionally unfitted to cope with. 'Where is my millionaire?' she wailed. But one day she reappeared in very good spirits having, she announced, just come upon a specimen who would do extremely well for the time being. A luxurious Daimler was now placed at our disposal – I say *our*, for to some extent I shared in Isadora's good fortune. With no more taxi fares to be paid, I could now, without afterthought, agree to an excursion after the theatre or of a morning. I knew of a good old-fashioned inn at Hampton Court where the cheer was good. I have hinted that Isadora's tastes were no more ascetic than my own at that time. However divided we might be in some respects, over a roast chicken and a bottle of good wine we were as one. The Hampton Court resort had only one drawback: there was absolutely no *réclame* to be gained there. Even after openly engaging a private room for our meal, we were never once interrupted or pursued by fans or photographers.

Isadora had established a school of dancing for children in Moscow. Her presence was needed there and she departed by air. I would have accompanied her as she suggested but, as usual, I had work which kept me. A good thing in itself, no doubt, in some circumstances industry makes a poor excuse and is best kept dark. And so, whatever my motives, I left them to be guessed. I was in Paris when the news came of the fatal accident at Nice. There was a memorial ceremony held in Paris which I should have attended, but, always shy of public demonstrations, I missed it. So ended my acquaintance with Isadora Duncan, the dancing Wonder of the World.

Actors and Actresses

IT HAS been said by a good judge 'All the World's a stage and all the men and women merely players'. But why *merely*? Play-acting is the essence of life. Everybody tries to act a part and thus extend himself in space. Unfortunately many have been allotted unsuitable roles in which they cannot possibly do themselves justice. This is a common complaint, and due partly to native incompetence and partly to the carelessness of an over-worked Producer. But there is still a chance for these misfits. Let them exceed themselves in inadequacy and they will end by making a triumph of failure! It should not be too difficult since they always have the looking-glass to guide them. 'Nothing succeeds like excess.'

Children are born mimes: even their shyness can be assumed and used as a means of display. Cats and dogs, too, when young, constantly resort to make-believe – sham fights, wrestling, ratting, bird catching, and all such fun. They seem almost human, as we say, like monkeys who also run us close when it comes to action. Hence our verb 'to ape'.

But the proof of our superiority lies in our ability to disguise ourselves convincingly and impersonate somebody else. Failure to do so provides the stock-in-trade of comedy; tragedy, on the other hand, depends on the degree of success we attain in this line. The ridiculous misunderstandings of the one are matched by the heroic cross-purposes of the other, and to each the element of duplicity is common. Hence we deduce the rule that deception is as the breath of life – that is, on the stage of course.

But I find I have wandered into the theatre now, where we see the world boiled down to a convenient size; the actors, somewhat enlarged and provided with masks, try to look natural while declaiming, in surroundings of a fascinating improbability, lines which, taken as a whole, with perhaps an occasional effort by the orchestra, combine to conjure up the illusion of reality or the shifting phantasmagoria of our dreams.

I used to think actors (and actresses), when off the stage, must be mentally vacant: living only fully in their parts, they would, I thought, be pretty dead outside them. Nothing of the kind! Actors are often better off the stage than on. They are still acting, of course, but in their own role. This allows them plenty of time for rehearsal, and, being naturally ambitious, they make the most of it. As nearly all people are slightly asymmetrical, each has to decide for himself which is the better side to lay stress on, and dispose himself accordingly. 'L'Art,' said Prosper Mérimée, 'c'est l'exagération à propos.' But under-emphasis is also important, and a good actor will employ both devices when necessary. This discreet interplay of accent constitutes style. Sacha Guitry certainly had it, as I observed for myself at one of du Maurier's luncheons at the Garrick Club. In his case the result was a genial naturalism, for which, even if it was assumed, I fell: just as one applauds a piece of trickery by a skilful conjurer, who leaves one both incredulous and delighted.

Sacha Guitry's professional partner, Yvonne Printemps, went further. As she spoke to me, while facing the light, her open mouth permitted me to examine its interior, and, to my astonishment, I realized this exquisite sound-box had not been neglected in the process of make up, for its nacreous surfaces repeated in all its nicety the delicate magenta of her lips! Again I fell, but this time with a more marked and lasting concussion.

Gerald du Maurier's style, an urbane and highly wrought genre, served him equally well on and off the stage. There was no need to vary his technique which, in each case, provided a perfect medium for his limited purposes. Though, as he told me, each movement cost him months of thought, experiment and elaboration, the outcome was always a triumph of subtle verisimilitude, and, like the grapes of Apelles, might be pecked by the hungry birds of criticism, but never punctured. His artful economy in the use of the sincerity motif alone was almost enough to take one in.

Though I have had little to do directly with the stage, I have had the good luck to meet many of the profession, and, at the instigation of Charles B. Cochran, did undertake the decor of two plays which he produced, *The Silver Tassie* by Sean O'Casey, for which I designed the principal scene, and *The Boy David* by Sir James Barrie. The first went very well, in spite of some short-comings in production, but the second came to grief. I had taken a great deal of trouble with the more ambitious possibilities which Barrie's play offered. My principal scene, a rocky landscape of Judea, was very well carried out, after a great deal of trouble, and when properly illuminated I thought it looked magnificent. I have never been to Palestine, but the late Lord Melchett, who was familiar with it, told me when he saw my designs in the studio that I had exactly captured the character of the country. I had provided a dark and lowering sky, with immense rocks in the foreground, from which descended a slender waterfall, giving rise to the brook from the bed of which David chose the pebbles he was to sling at Goliath. The water presented no difficulty to the technicians, or if it did they overcame it. How charmingly it glittered as it fell! I had finished my share of the work within a week or two of the opening, when for some reason unknown to me Cochran found it necessary to change his producer. On the first night a tragic surprise awaited me when the curtain rose on my cherished landscape. Gone was the stormy sky. It had been replaced by a plain white backcloth! Gone was my waterfall, an indispensable adjunct to the design. Gone, in consequence, was the unity and character of the whole picture. As for the other scenes, they had been repainted by another hand, without, as far

as I could judge, being in any way improved. I hurried to the bar
and stayed there. This play was a complete flop from the start,
and I wasn't sorry. But I *was* sorry for poor Elisabeth Bergner,
who had been turning head-over-heels so playfully and indus-
triously during so many rehearsals, and all for this fiasco!

It dawned on me too late that I had neither the technique nor
the physical attributes for this sort of work, apart from the
question of my artistic ability. Work necessitating collaboration,
as in this case, calls for the authority of a field-marshal coupled
with the moral and material equipment of a gangster. Hitler, who
as we know shone in both capacities, besides being a bit of an
artist, had at least a good run for our money, and if he failed in
the end he had only himself to blame, since there was no one
above him to accuse. I, who at least had Mr Cochran over me,
certainly did lodge a complaint, but that amiable and adventurous
being, secure behind his cohort of Young Ladies, succeeded –
though with some difficulty – in appeasing me; his apologies were
reinforced by a satisfactory cheque. I am glad to say we remained
friends but not collaborators.

J. M. Barrie had not been helpful. He found my view of
Bethlehem topographically incorrect. It was. I had imagined an
austere little hill-town, decorated with olive trees, terraces and
perhaps a few cypress trees such as are found in Provence, and
probably, I thought, in Palestine too, for the two countries are in
much the same zone. But Barrie produced a sketch by a friend
of his of the place as it really is, or at any rate as this artist saw it,
being on the spot. In the middle distance one detected an insignificant village with what might have been a church, set in the
dreariest of landscapes, of a flat and muddy green. In spite of this
evidence and Barrie's insistence, I preferred my own idea and
stuck to it: for one thing, it was better 'theatre'. Upon reflection
I have begun to think this conflict of opinion was the cause of the
subsequent mutilations of my designs. C.B. was not the man to

betray a friend at the behest of the author of the play, and that author J. M. Barrie himself.

As a youth I saw Henry Irving perform several times at the Lyceum. The tall black figure plunged on to the stage as if propelled by destiny. He might be inarticulate with passion, but his voice preserved the poetic tempo none the less distinctly. His exquisite gestures could be those of a saint, a warrior or a king. The nobility of his progression deathwards might perhaps be matched in a fresco by Giotto.

My sister Gwen and I went to see an Arthurian drama in which Irving figured, and on reaching our lodgings, still under the spell of the Master, I seized a heavy walking stick, raised it above my head, while reciting appropriate lines, and smashed the chandelier! Excalibur had struck again ...

Ellen Terry was one of those rare women who, reversing the usual rule, gain in liveliness with every year. When she came to live in Chelsea, though by other standards an old woman, she seemed to have reached the summit of vivacity. Demure young girls, relying on delayed action, discharge their amorous missiles unobtrusively, with an eye to catch their quarry later, as defence-less they lie in bed and dream; but older ones like Ellen (if there be any such), having less time to spare, engage at once in frank aggression: careless of their dwindling ammunition, it's hit or miss with them. Practically invulnerable themselves, they laugh at opposition for they have Death on their side. In my own case, rather than join a queue of corpses, I surrendered without a blow.

Gwen Farrar, who later lived in the house mentioned above, was a genius of a different order. Of course she belonged to a very different world from that of her happier predecessor. Hers was the Faery world; the world of cacodemons and pigwidgeons; the world of the unblest. She was the up-rooted one, the change-ling, the proud pilgarlic, the play-girl of the moon, and she had a voice like a coal-heaver.

I have never cultivated coal-heavers; I prefer to keep out of their way; not that I have anything against them morally, but I find their make-up repellent; to me it is affected without being witty. Unlike the cunning maquillage of the clown, it is based on no ancient tradition but seems to be purely haphazard and misses the morbid appeal of the nigger-minstrel who does at any rate give tongue to the inarticulate yearnings of the holiday maker, in strains of a transcendent if transatlantic vulgarity. I welcome the rare street-cry, but the hoarse call of the coalman does nothing to lighten the gloom of the back street.

Gwen Farrar's voice, when first she turned it on in my hearing, gave me an enormous shock. I hesitated between laughter and dismay. Could this be the real Gwen Farrar? If so, what could she have been drinking? Was she merely doing a turn? With actors you never know ...

The fact is, as I realized later, she was only indulging in one of her private impersonations; but it was a favourite one and seemed to come quite naturally to this perverse and adorable being. I soon got to love it. Come back and talk to me, Gwen!

I was overcome by Eleonora Duse. She was acting in a play by Ibsen. The intensity of emotion which it was her business to suppress communicated itself to me. I found myself in an exactly parallel situation. As a Welshman, it would have been natural and proper to give full vent to my feelings, but my English veneer made such an exhibition unthinkable. This resulted in a familiar and painful dichotomy which could only be relieved by a pistol shot. I was astonished to discover that Italians are not, as I thought, all born actors. The Duse's entourage was most inadequate. But perhaps her countrymen are only first rate at heroics; in this play, conspicuously apart from the principal role, no such opportunities presented themselves.

I think I can claim to have had a share in the eventual success of the Sicilian Players on their first appearance in London. There must still be some who remember Grasso and his company. Their season started badly. Moved by some mysterious impulse, I attended the opening performance. The theatre was practically empty: my applause must have seemed disproportionate but I persisted; gathering a few friends, we constituted ourselves an unprofessional *claque* and night after night created a terrible din after each act. Gradually our exertions began to bear fruit; our enthusiasm spread, more and more people began to trickle in, till after a strenuous week or two the theatre filled itself nightly. The battle was won!

Walter Sickert joined in with the Partisans, and with his knowledge of Italian made the acquaintance of some of the Sicilians, especially Mimi Agulia, the principal lady. She was persuaded to come to his studio to pose for some drawings. This brilliant little actress said of herself and her confrères: 'We just try to be natural.' She was modesty itself. Everyone insisted that I should present her with my drawing. I did so. It was hung in the foyer of the theatre till the end of the season, when the company departed with it to South America. I would very much like that drawing back, if it exists, or to have a photograph of it.

The return of the Sicilians brought disappointment, at any rate for me. As usual, success had spoiled them. Unnecessary elaboration had taken the place of simplicity; a more showy but less talented leading lady had been substituted for Agulia; even Grasso had lost some of his pristine innocence and swagger.

When the Jewish Vilna Players gave a season in London I became a frequent spectator at their performances, and so did Sickert. Though I had no Yiddish, such was the excellence of the acting that it was easy to follow the gist of what was said. The weird and disturbing play, *Der Dybbuk*, above all enthralled me. The terrifying phenomenon of 'possession' is a rarity in this country, but not I think unknown. I wonder one of our own playwrights has not made use of this motif.

93

Finishing Touches

I once saw Sarah Bernhardt, but not on the stage; it was at the entrance to a theatre. She lay on a litter, having had a leg amputated recently. A play was in progress, but the divine Sarah hadn't come to see a play: she had come *to be* seen. The auditorium was in darkness. She demanded that the lights be turned on. The manager, with infinite apologies, refused to do this, for the play was in progress. Furious, she was carried out again, with the face of a Gorgon. Was the manager right or wrong? A nice point.

The stage used to be well represented at the old Eiffel Tower in Percy Street. This restaurant in its palmy days used sometimes to become over-crowded of an evening. On one such night Stulick, the patron, implored me to help him keep out any new-comers, for there was hardly standing room and the waiters were distraught. Accordingly I went to the front entrance and managed to dissuade some fresh applicants from entering. Unfortunately one of the oldest and most esteemed clients turned up. It was none other than that prince of comedy, Ronald Squire. What was I to do? I could only explain the situation and stand firm. Squire's indignation was only matched by my discomfort. How willingly I would have given up my chair had I not been inextricably involved with some guests that evening. I returned to my more legitimate responsibilities in no happy mood. Ronnie, being an unique combination of artist, saint and philosopher, and with, I suspect, more than a touch of second-sight as well, remains in spite of our contretemps my very good friend and hero.

At that time Robert Newton had not attained his present eminence. His manly beauty was unenhanced by the costly accoutrements of Californian fashion which now he wears so bravely. But Bob was always brave; brave, simple and above-board, even when under the weather. This man of many parts, in his good fortune careless; with the great heart of adolescent humanity beating more quickly at his nod, may even in his heyday profit by a word of warning. Such a warning I take it upon myself to administer (a septuagenarian must be indulged): 'The Gods have conferred on you, my dear Bob, among other gifts, a generous allowance of Sentiment. If you would enjoy this abundance to the full, you would do well to use it sparingly and with an eye to the stomach, for it might come back on you – or worse, on some innocent person in your neighbourhood. To vary the metaphor: when running a race, with such a horse as Sentiment under you, the strongest and the most vicious in your stable, beware lest you come a cropper or be run away with. Let your steed always feel the rein, dear boy, but not the spur; by keeping well within the not too exiguous limits of Dickensian Melodrama (though I myself favour a narrower course) you and your noble beast are bound to romp in – winners every time!'

Esmé Percy, a pure Elizabethan if ever there was one, though he never told me his age, must be a good deal older than he looks, though not so old as I am. Perhaps, like me, he has forgotten the precise date of his birth, which at a guess I would place somewhere in the sixteenth century. Although I am his senior, the gap between our years is not so wide as to have divided us as children, though it would doubtless be enough to have thrown into relief, more than it would today, the precocious gravity of the older child as compared with the gay ebullience of his playmate; but as there is not the slightest evidence that any such association took place, I will at once abandon a utopian speculation and turn to facts, or rather possibilities.

At the period suggested, I might well have been a simple shepherd boy watching his flock upon the rough pastures of Prescelly, for it was from these windy uplands that my forbears sprang, without, it appears, landing in any instance far from the take-off. But clues to such activities are scarce; mountain mists make exploration hazardous and the trail to the Ancestral Stones has long been overgrown.

To beguile the reader for a little while, let me by a process of association reconstruct the story of my meeting with the distinguished Player named above, and, in a new perspective, place the event midway between an almost legendary past and a too photographic present.

For this purpose, borrowing the licence usually reserved to poets, I will add a flavouring of historical colour by the introduction of persons, circumstances and names known to everybody in connection with the period chosen, and entitle the result:

An Elizabethan Interlude

When, having won a scholarship, I was sent to Oxford to be civilized, I found Jesus College simply pullulating with my compatriots, few of whom knew much English, and in some cases only indifferent Welsh. Welded together at last under the common tyranny of a masterful fellow countrywoman, each tribesman brought out his pedigree entitling him without a doubt to a seat at the Round Table, a choice of the attendant virgins and an unlimited supply of metheglin. Arthur had come again, it seemed, or was due to return at any moment. In this hot-airy atmosphere my studies languished, my behaviour worsened, and when at last sent down, I came to London to seek a job. After a time, as luck would have it, I succeeded.

It was a pleasant change to leave my filthy lodging in Shoreditch and come to live in Chelsea, then a village, though I missed the Playhouses to which I was addicted; 'The Theatre' or 'The Curtain' which, with the new 'Rose' across the river, had been my favourite haunts of an afternoon before the plague drove people out of London, were of course shut for the time being, and the Players for the most part had taken to the road. But I was at least fairly safe in Chelsea, and with other fugitives at no loss for company. Besides, on becoming tutor to the children of a lady of substance, I was not without means wherewith to pay my

standing in the local taverns on the river bank, of which, considering the limited population in normal times, there were perhaps too many.

It is noticeable that danger adds an extra zest to life, and at the time I am speaking of the proximity of death, in a most loathsome form, induced a certain recklessness and appetite for pleasure which ordinarily would have been judged reprehensible and even vulgar.

My employer, subject like all young people (and indeed to some extent the old) to the general urge, having been left in affluence as a result of the industry and forethought of her late husband (a highly respected and substantial wool merchant), had already begun to entertain somewhat largely, when, having been presented by a common friend, I made her acquaintance. Touched by her beauty and amiability, I soon became a frequent guest at her house, where, having some facility for dancing and conversation, I was made welcome. The defencelessness of this lady began to cause me concern, for I knew the village to be crowded with strangers from the city, many of whom being but ruffians and tricksters, out as much to line their pockets as to save their skins; among them too, and they the worst, were some disguised as gentlemen.

Our acquaintance developing into friendship, at my hostess's suggestion I readily agreed to take upon myself the instruction of her children. For greater convenience I was lent a room in her spacious house where I might sleep and do some work of my own, had I the mind. This arrangement pleased me greatly, for apart from my own profit, it empowered me to keep an eye on the visitors and, if need be, discourage those I deemed unworthy or worse. I could thus serve my young Mistress better than she bargained for, and without her knowledge. Having become a trifle arrogant in her good looks and enviable circumstances, the widow would have ridiculed any suggestion of her incompetence to take care of herself, and certainly would have scorned any offer of protection from so insignificant a person as myself, although my occasional interventions were not ill-timed nor were they disapproved, as I could see.

The party was breaking up; many of the guests had gone home, but a few enthusiasts remained, and the musicians, though half-fuddled, still played on. I was standing at the improvised bar contrived in a corner of the ballroom, when two newcomers were announced. I caught a familiar name, that of the Player Esmé Percy, whom I had often admired; I had supposed him to be absent in Wiltshire with the Earl of Pembroke's men. These tardy revellers, having paid their respects to the hostess, now joined me at the bar. Vague introductions took place. I did not catch the name of Percy's companion. The two had just come up the river from Southwark. It seemed they had been spending a considerable time in that quarter, especially at the drink-shop in the Clink belonging to one Will Shakspere. I had heard of this man, who was well known in theatrical circles and reputed rich. Besides his work as prompter and sometimes actor, he was dispenser of robes and costumes, of which it was said he had a fine collection, and he dealt in Plays, too, and would employ hard-up writers of talent and even genius to emend, alter and patch up these for him, when he would sell them as his own. This wily factotum, among other activities, was said to run a smart brothel in Blackfriars. I had heard all this gossip myself.

Though I overheard the name of Shakspere mentioned more than once by Percy, it was mostly in ridicule; his companion appearing to be uninterested in or impatient of the topic. A strange fellow this, I thought; dressed with great simplicity in black, in contrast to the fashionable elaborateness of the actor's attire, his style was that of a gentleman, but I found his manners insupportable: disdainful, truculent and provocative. I began to consider the propriety of exerting my privilege as chucker-out, when, to my astonishment, an extraordinary change took place in this humorist's demeanour; whether the effects of Master Shakspere's bad sack had worn off or taken a new turn, or whether my Mistress's superior liquor had wrought a miracle, in any case the unknown, drawing in his horns, now apologized for his ill-manners, and addressed me with the utmost modesty and solicitude. To my surprise my resentment vanished instantly under the illumination of the stranger's smile, and, as I listened to his voice, my heart began to burn: where had I heard that voice before? As my eyes met his, I trembled, for in them I seemed to discern the majesty, the sorrow and the understanding of – a god in exile … ! Inexpressibly moved, I would have cast myself at his feet, for I had lost all sense of time, identity and my surroundings, when Percy broke the spell of this enchantment: 'Come,' he said, 'the tide has turned, we must go back.'

The ballroom was empty. As in a dream I saw them to the door, where the stranger, throwing his cloak about him, murmured a good night and disappeared. Before the Player could follow, I seized him by the arm: 'Esmé,' I cried, 'tell me, who is that man?'

'What,' he replied, and in a whisper, 'didn't you guess? Why, that is The Poet … !'

Portraits of Prime Ministers

Winston Churchill

I haven't painted many Prime Ministers. I can think of only three or four colonials and our own Ramsay MacDonald; but I have *drawn* A. J. Balfour and Mr Winston Churchill. The former came to sit for me in Fitzroy Street at the behest of his sister. I had always admired this statesman. His philosophy of doubt appealed to me and, what is more important, so did his appearance and manner. Having placed him in a comfortable chair, I set to and completed the drawing within an hour. Whereupon, waking up, Mr Balfour glanced at my effort, and remarking 'A very fine piece of work', disappeared.

Mr Churchill was much more difficult. I first met him at John Lavery's studio a good many years ago. He had brought some pictures to show which I thought commendable. After that I used to see him now and then at the luncheon parties Mrs Valentine Fleming gave at 'Turner's House', Chelsea. 'Turner's House' had gone through drastic changes since the great painter lodged and died there under the name of Booth. Booth was really the name of his landlady (who was a widow): it was at once adopted by the artist. This simplified matters, I suppose; anyhow 'Old Billy Booth' was known to all the ragamuffins in the neighbourhood who used to pursue him with their gibes.

The little house has been transformed since then, and a large studio built at the back by a man I knew at the Slade called Balfour, and my future friend Lionel Curtis. Later, during the tenancy of Mrs Fleming, the nice little beer house next door called The Aquatic Stores, which I found so sympathetic, unfortunately lost its licence and was then taken over and embodied in 'Turner's

House'. In spite of the plaque on the front which commemorates the name of its former august tenant, it is certain that if Joseph Mallord William Turner came back, he would have had some difficulty in recognizing his now transformed little lodging house on the river-side, and it is most unlikely that he would feel at home at Mrs Fleming's luncheon parties, even if he were ever invited to one of these distinguished gatherings. No; for him the simpler and perhaps grosser amenities of Wapping were to be preferred, and it was thither he was accustomed to repair for recreation of a Saturday night.

On a visit to the House of Commons one day as a guest of the late member for King's Norton, Mr Raymond Blackburn, we approached the Prime Minister and I raised the question of a drawing. A picture had been long mooted, but involved as he was in affairs of state he agreed to sit for a drawing only and a date was fixed. On the day indicated, a car was sent by the P.M. to pick me up at Tite Street. My daughter Poppet and Mr Blackburn joined me by arrangement, and we all three were driven down to Mr Churchill's house in Kent, where we were received by young Captain Soames, our host's son-in-law, Mrs Churchill, for whom I had the greatest regard, being unfortunately laid up with a cold. Presently the great man appeared in his 'siren suit' and the operation began. I soon discovered that my model, however efficient in other ways, was no great shakes at keeping still. My target turned out to be a moving one. But I had often drawn charming but restless children before, and was now to tackle a somewhat similar proposition. In this case, I was limited to a single sitting, so had to make the most of it. On the whole the result was not too bad, I thought, considering the difficulties in my way.

Luncheon was now served. Mr Churchill of course took the head of the table. His charming daughter, Mrs Soames, sat at my left. Mr Blackburn at the other end of the table faced the P.M., his fine eyes glowing with the love and adoration of an early Christian convert in the presence of his Saviour. My daughter, also a great fan of the P.M., sat opposite me. During the meal Mr Churchill entertained us with reminiscences of his school days and early manhood. It appeared that as a schoolboy he had never distinguished himself either at his books or in the playing field, but apparently he woke up a bit while serving as a soldier in the Sudan, especially on one occasion when a black warrior offered to transfix him with a spear, at Omdurman or somewhere. Young Lieutenant Churchill felt he had to get his in first, and you bet he did, though, mind you, he 'didn't like doing it'. Luncheon was over, but, spellbound, we still lingered over our coffee, which in my case had been reinforced by a generous share of the Prime Minister's brandy. I fully appreciated this mark of favour and noted with approval that the member for King's Norton had not been similarly honoured. Our host's easy flow of reminiscence had gradually come to include our own times in its purview: his passing reference to the bombing of Nagasaki and Hiroshima, for which, it seems, he shared some responsibility, provided me, I thought, with a legitimate opening for an expression of regret that this atrocity should have been perpetrated by our allies. 'But it may have saved thousands of lives,' declared the statesman sharply. 'Perhaps,' I replied, 'but our soldiers are not expected to take shelter behind the corpses of non-combatants, nor are they accustomed to buy immunity at the price of the blood and agony of helpless women, old men and children. Besides, the war was virtually over and … ' but well before I had got as far as this I saw that I had exceeded my time allowance, and Mr Churchill had already entered on a further chapter of his memoirs. I was much too slow for this agile septuagenarian.

Before leaving, I assisted at a demonstration of a new kind of paint Mr Churchill had taken to using. It was a Swiss production inaccurately called 'Tempera'. Put up in tubes, the stuff could be squeezed out and diluted with water. Setting up a good-sized canvas, my instructor who had now recovered his normal good spirits, attacked it vigorously with his new medium – and, quickly, a mountainous landscape appeared, complete with a lake and a chalet. The latter feature requiring a window, this was instantly supplied with one straight right from the shoulder, a master stroke! Before I left, Mr Churchill loaded me with a parcel of his new pigments to take home, and added a bunch of suitable brushes too, but alas, by the time I was ready to try the colours, I found they had solidified. As a final gesture, the kindly old gentleman handed me an outsize cigar; in fact, I was given a very good send-off.

'The Soul's Awakening'

If Ramsay MacDonald in his day could never be said to rival Mr Churchill as a National, or rather International institution, nor, as a mere Parliamentarian, hold a candle to Mr Churchill in pugnacity, perspicacity, wit, and general God-damnedness; yet he, in one series of tests at any rate, showed himself the better man.

I am not concerned here with politics, but only with a matter of manners, and then only in so far as they affect me professionally. I have mentioned Mr Churchill's strange inability to keep still while I was trying to draw him. He was evidently unhappy under my scrutiny. How else to explain these fits and starts, these visits to the mirror, this preoccupation with the window curtains, and the nervous fidgeting with his jowl? All this agitation didn't help me in the least, and with only an hour or two at my disposal (without counting a rest now and then), it was all I could do to keep calm myself and avoid an explosion. But I was aware of the alternative which faced me. You can draw a man, or you can punch him; you cannot do both ...

Finishing Touches

Although in the business of portraiture, the artist must be prepared to accept every deviation from the normal, and even perhaps accentuate them, in so far as they afford a clue to the elucidation of character, he will require to some extent the collaboration of his model, if he is to bring out the more pleasing aspect of the latter's personality. It has been found that the practice of an attentive yet easy immobility best assures this, together with a resolve on the part of the subject to look his best, or what he thinks is his best, which comes to much the same thing and is equally revealing. Whatever may be thought of the work now under consideration, its shortcomings cannot be blamed on Mr MacDonald, who, following my suggestions, took every risk and stuck it out to the end.

Moved by some mysterious premonition, I posed my P.M. with his head turned over his shoulder and almost in profile, while an open book occupied his hands in the centre; his eyes, like those of a visionary, being directed upwards and far away. Thus I obtained a suggestion, less of the dour and horny-handed champion of the People than of the dreamy knight-errant, dedicated to the overthrow of dragons and the rescue of distressed damsels held captive by them. A stray lock of hair breaking the too severe contour of his brow, provided, I thought, an appropriate note of romantic informality. I could not help feeling, though, that my sitter was not wholly reassured by my reading of his character. As he examined it during the rests, I observed the beginnings of a wry smile struggling with an expression of perplexity, as if there were something odd and perhaps important on the tip of his tongue which yet eluded capture.

'There is a well-known picture,' he remarked at last, 'which your portrait reminds me of, but I cannot recall its name.'

Instantly Sant's masterpiece sprang to my mind. 'Do you mean "The Soul's Awakening"?' I asked. 'Yes, that's it,' he cried, ' "The Soul's Awakening"!' We both had a good laugh at this discovery.

Decidedly, MacDonald was not entirely without humour, though the responsibilities of high office sometimes got in its way. A little less *empressement* would have served his purposes better, and have reassured his friends while worrying his enemies equally.

George Moore's funeral coincided with the completion of the portrait, and, as we had both known the deceased, at MacDonald's suggestion, we attended the last rites at Golder's Green together. On this occasion I was unimpressed by the preliminaries incidental to the cremation of an unbeliever, and after seeing the case containing the corpse, propelled by some hidden mechanism, disappear through an orifice in the wall, I made for the open air with much relief. As we made our exit the appearance of a group of clergy startled me. I had forgotten that such types existed. Byzantine in character, they were at the same time not unlike the stylized figures found in early Saxon art and quite unbelievable. I had thought of a drink at the Café Royal, but affairs of state, no doubt, claimed my politician, and I saw the last of him standing on the door-step of an important-looking house, his fine head slightly bowed in thought, with his erect figure, half-turned towards the public, showing a graceful curve. I was reminded at once of the stately occupants of Parliament Square, but I had to admit the line of his trousers belied this comparison, and, although his boots, so blunt and workaday, seemed to shine with more than their usual lustre, this was probably an effect of the rather theatrical sunset which was blazing in the west, as if in acclamation of my model, or (it occurred to me), more likely in honour of George Moore, by now just about due at the turnstile of the Irish Valhalla.

Asides

PERFECT physical union, though never to be despised, is soon forgotten unless constantly renewed; but complete fusion of body and spirit, ah! that indeed is rare, but it is remembered for ever!

* * *

Those fellows who think they can dominate a woman by bawling at her will soon find they are mistaken. Such conduct is ill-bred besides being the lowest form of Noel Cowardice.

* * *

To Robbie Ross and Reggie Turner fell the job of cleaning up after Oscar exploded. They told me it was awful, like picking up confetti, and they had to use their hat-pins!

* * *

When Wyndham Lewis got Bozie Douglas to sit for him, he hadn't seen his Lordship before, or he might have thought better of it. After the first sitting he asked me what he ought to do about Bozie's nose. I told him, of course, to make it a bit bigger; but Lewis demurred: he said he had to draw the line somewhere.

* * *

It's all very well for Lewis to issue a clarion call to Artists at this time of day to stop abstracting before they go 'over the precipice' as he puts it. But I think my son Robin went further than this about twenty years ago. He went to Paris anyhow, and there succeeded in pushing *his* abstractions to the point of complete invisibility: he framed the results and hung 'em up in his studio, where they are still not to be seen, even by Lewis, unfortunately. It is true Robin himself *has* gone over the edge in a way, but I haven't lost faith in him yet. He isn't dead and I expect a call from the depths at any moment.

*   *   *

Sir John Rothenstein seems to have inherited some of his father's pugnacity. But when Will knocked Charles Conder down, the latter wasn't in training, and anyhow his leg-work was never considered satisfactory, although I know he could make good mileage, given a sufficient motif. None of that lot were really athletic, except perhaps Robert Sherard; but then he simply *lived* on something called 'Vi-Cocoa', if one can believe the advertisements of the period. Will Rothenstein was certainly quick enough on his feet when it was a question of the last helping of *Cœur a la Crème* after lunch; he was no good at drinking though, it always gave him jaundice. As for Max Beerbohm, perhaps the less said the better, but he always looked to me as if he'd had enough.

*   *   *

'All art is a memory of age-old things, dark things, whose fragments live on in the artist.' – Paul Klee.

Dylan Thomas and Company[1]

THESE sketches of three men I have known and admired make no claim to exact portraiture, though they do aim at registering as accurately as possible some aspects of them I have noted during our long and fairly intimate acquaintance. For the rest, I have done nothing more than avail myself of the first privilege of a friend, which is to speak with complete frankness, combined with a touch of malice when necessary. No attempt at embellishment will be found, I hope, nor anything like defamation, which would only recoil on my own head.

The late Nina Hamnett (who, like me, came from Tenby) introduced me to the Fitzroy Tavern – a largish pub on a corner of Charlotte Street. It was kept by a Jewish family, whose head, an elderly man of the name of Kleinfeld, I became friendly with; he used to teach me some words of Yiddish, a few of which I remember (such as *muzzle* for luck), and others may crop up in my memory when I have no need for them.

Mr Kleinfeld knew all about 'Der Dybbuk', a terrifying spirit which had been the subject of a play by the company of the Vilna Players which I used to frequent, as did Sickert. Mr Kleinfeld saw nothing funny in 'Der Dybbuk', nor did I or anybody who had seen this play so wonderfully acted in Yiddish; but Mr Klein-feld, though he had the simplicity of a child, was no fool. If I knew the Yiddish for 'gentleman' I would use it to describe Mr Kleinfeld.

A custom at the Fitzroy Tavern was to collect enough money to send the local poor children to the seaside every year. The clients contributed towards this, if they liked, by throwing their

[1] First published in *The Sunday Times* Magazine Section on September 28th, 1958.

money, wrapped up in paper and attached to darts (provided by the management), up to the ceiling, to which the missives stuck if correctly aimed. Charity thus became a popular game of skill. Nina Hamnett, although she might often miss the target herself, encouraged this practice, for she was the soul of generosity, as many a forlorn artist of Montparnasse in search of a drink, a meal and a doss-down could testify.

One evening I entered the tavern to find it unusually crowded. There were many faces which were strange to me, but Nina's was inescapable as she tottered around for a refill and seemed mysteriously to be in more than one place at a time.

There was a sprinkling of music-hall comedians, with that curious air of unreality about them which these artists always wear when off the stage. Perhaps this was due to their having washed their faces, for they carried no make-up or very little; but the knowing look of the 'profession' gave them away (as it was meant to do). Their superior knowledge of the world could not and should not be disguised. 'Hullo, Augustus,' says one veteran. 'You're growing old.' 'Yes,' says I, absently; 'but I'll never catch up with you, Arthur.'

I found a seat some distance from the counter, which was inaccessible except by the language of signs, but there were willing hands to fetch me my drink. In the hurly-burly words were indistinguishable to me, but the peculiar *miaulement* of a group of epicenes could be recognized clearly, and nearer at hand the cultured ejaculations of Cambridge vied with the somewhat blurred but no less authoritative accents of South Wales.

My companion whispered in my ear, 'Dylan Thomas!' Could she be right? She could, for at my side I found the Welsh poet established. It was our first meeting. I lost no time in ordering drinks all round to mark the occasion. As beer seemed to be the order of the day, I wisely forwent my usual double rum and brandy in favour of the popular pint.

The other personality of our little group, Mr William Empson, although at this time enjoying none of the Welshman's notoriety, played no second fiddle but, as if under the spell of the *hwyl*, or divine afflatus, gave one at moments the illusion of rising like a bird above the ground! To achieve the Top of the World is worth taking a risk, no doubt, but I wouldn't advise lesser men than Empson to try it. I was moved greatly by his performance, being something of an old mountaineer myself, and on a lower plane may call myself one of his fans.

In a distant corner Professor Haldane might have been observed. Notebook in hand, he appeared to be in deep thought, but his Nietzschian features showed on this occasion no irradiation proper to an amateur of the *Gaya Scienza*; on the contrary, it seemed that he might be murmuring to himself: 'Là où vous voyez des choses idéales, moi je vois ... des choses humaines, hélas! trop humaines!' I don't suppose any of the specimens he contemplated were in any sense 'idéal', but that some of them were 'trop humaines', or perhaps not human enough, is quite likely. The professor was possibly engaged on a new anthropological study, to be entitled 'How the Poor Live'.

My own new acquaintances made a happy contrast, very dissimilar structurally. Empson's features recalled a late Michelangelo based on some recently unearthed and slightly damaged antiquity, while Dylan's face was round and his nose snub. His rather prominent eyes were a little veiled and his curly hair was red, or auburn rather. A pleasant and slightly sardonic smile registered amusement and, I think, satisfaction. If you could have substituted an ice for the glass of beer he held you might have mistaken him for a happy schoolboy out on the spree.

When he spoke I was astonished by the purity of his vowels, but then I remembered that the best English is heard in Carmarthenshire. In spite, as I noticed later, of his being tone-deaf, his voice had a beautiful resonance and, thanks to his Welsh-speaking parents, his accent was just enough to lend his speech an additional note of character and distinction.

In spite of his upbringing he had little or no Welsh himself, but he would readily break into the mixed dialect when telling a story or indulging in local *facetiae*. Even his English was limited, and a word of four syllables might baffle him. He had no French or Latin, of course, and showed interest in no other literatures but English, in which he was, however, far from being widely read, apart from the 'thrillers', in which he was so well versed. Dickens to him came next to Shakespeare, and it is doubtful if he knew any other English writers unless by hearsay.

He professed the usual sympathy for the underdog, for he was one himself, and at one time, like many other simpletons, he was persuaded to join the Communist Party, though he had no knowledge of sociology or of any political theories from Plato to Poujade.

Later, however, on being ordered to make himself the poetic mouthpiece of Moscow, he had the sense to quit the 'Party', and after that attached himself to no other political movement, unless his propensity for sponging on his better-to-do acquaintances could be dignified by such a name. In any case he could always be relied upon as a borrower, and such was his magnetism that few would grudge him the price of a drink, let alone free residence for a month or two. As for food, he seemed indifferent to it, but was familiar with several little clubs where drinks could be procured between or after hours.

Perhaps the chief difference between a writer and a painter is that the latter depends so much upon the weather in this climate. If he stays up late he is conscious of wasting his time, for it may mean getting up late next day and perhaps missing a valuable ray of sunlight. A writer, and especially a poet, suffers from no such anxieties: for him breakfast may be deferred indefinitely. Furnished with a fountain-pen, an exercise-book and a packet of fags he brings his studio with him. Among friends he feels at his best at night and the later the friendlier.

I was always glad to meet Dylan in the day-time but often gladder still to see the last of him at night, when his magic had departed, leaving nothing but the interminable reverberations of the alcoholic. It is possible that some of his grassiest verses originated in the fetid atmosphere of a pub or a night-club. But I have never been a student of his poems, and though I have read (and enjoyed) some of them, not a single line remains in my memory.

This, however, means nothing derogatory, for my memory is often defective. Yet, when put to it, as at school, I was able to beat every competitor at memorizing Walter Scott (and by more than a canto!). But on those occasions I had the incentive of annoying the Headmaster, who had seen fit publicly to asperse my veracity and morals and even throw doubt on my chances of salvation after an early death in a mad-house. When, shortly afterwards, this pedagogue cut his throat in a railway carriage, he was probably as unaware of the power of the Evil Eye as he had been of my capacity for learning poetry by heart, let alone truth-telling, etc.

But to return to Dylan Thomas. I went to a memorial performance of his *Under Milk Wood*, and other works, where I was provided with a seat in a box already crowded. Half way through the performance, most of which I couldn't hear, I made my escape to seek out Caitlin Thomas, whom I knew to be present. I succeeded in finding her.

Seizing my arm, she said, 'Come out of this – I've got a date to keep.' We got a taxi and were driven to a pub, where we found a group of her friends awaiting her. After a few drinks we went back to the theatre, in spite of Caitlin's delaying tactics: I wanted to say how-do-you-do to two or three of the actors whom I knew and admired, including Edith Evans and Emlyn Williams. I thought on meeting them that their reception of me lacked

12

14

15

warmth; I suppose they resented my furtive exit from the theatre with Caitlin, who had not disguised her contempt for the whole show.

I have read and listened to *Under Milk Wood* since. There is no trace of wit in this work. Some of the characterization was passable, for I thought I recognized a type or two from New Quay in Cardiganshire. But I did *not* recognize the so-called 'Gypsies': such unearthly dummies couldn't have taken in a policeman! The whole hotch-potch is a humourless travesty of popular life and is served up in a bowl of cold *cawl* in which large gobbets of false sentiment are embedded. Pouah!

In his rendering of Welsh life Dylan Thomas never got near the level of Caradoc Evans, a far more conscientious historian, who was of course reviled by his countrymen, for he exposed their vices unmercifully, as an artist must. Like God, he chastised those he loved (or at any rate their nearest relations), for every year he left his miserable employment to go back to his beloved country for a fortnight.

He asked me to go with him, and said that he would introduce me to some of 'the most beautiful girls in the world'. Unfortunately, I couldn't go just then and will always regret missing the opportunity of associating more closely with so fine a spirit as Caradoc and on such a quest!

After Dylan Thomas's marriage to Caitlin Macnamara, at which, having been by accident instrumental in bringing them together, I acted as second best man, they came now and then to stay at Caitlin's home between Fordingbridge and Ringwood. We frequently met, usually at Dylan's favourite pub in the latter town. Dylan had become a devotee of shove-ha'penny, a game to which I was (and am) addicted: he played well, too. I got him to sit for me twice, the second portrait being the more successful: provided with a bottle of beer he sat very patiently, which is more than I can say for several other distinguished people I could

H

name, and they not exactly teetotallers, either. He was not conceited and, though he could be pugnacious at moments, he and I never came to blows.

As for his life in America, a devoted and long-suffering American friend has written an admirable account of this, the poet's last deplorable phase, in *Dylan Thomas in America*, while Caitlin herself, not to be outdone, has recorded her later experiences as a widow in Italy with remarkable frankness, and some humour. Unlike Dylan, she is never guilty of sentimentality, and, while apparently in a perpetual state of disgust with the world in general, seems to have chosen instinctively the lowest and dirtiest dram-shop of a mining town in Elba as her refuge from it.

Whence comes this *nostalgie de la boue*? Hardly from her irreproachable Irish and French antecedents! The fact is that only in salt water can Caitlin find the purity and freedom she seeks. She swims well – is not her maiden name *Macnamara*, which (accommodating the genders) means: Daughter of the Son of the Sea? For a long time her father, Francis, did in fact keep a boat tied up in Galway Harbour, of his own design and rig, a boon, as Oliver Gogarty remarked, to the local washer-women ...

I would like to scotch the popular legend that Dylan Thomas was perpetually drunk, bawdy and licentious. In my experience he was none of these things. Under the threat of T.B. he certainly sought confidence and distraction in beer, but he could stomach more of this beverage than most people without getting sodden. He hated solitude and loved the atmosphere of a good pub or, in a lesser degree, a night-club, for he was always loth to go to bed. Perhaps towards morning he might grow repetitive and tiresome, but he was never gross himself, even if he had some droll stories to tell ...

One night at the Gargoyle I was sitting with him and the then proprietor, David Tennant. The latter, trying to draw him out, asked, 'Do you believe in multi-matrimony?' Dylan replied, 'No,

I don't, I believe in one wife only.' And he was very serious. But at that time he wasn't married, nor had he visited the U.S.A.

It was in New York that his system broke down. It was there that whisky, which he shunned in this country, played hell with his brain, with the dire results we know. And it was there that his poetic faculty deserted him completely, though he still did his stuff on the platform with tremendous success, and it was there that he re-wrote and finished *Under Milk Wood* which I have derided. The truth is that Dylan was at the core a typical Welsh puritan and nonconformist gone wrong. He was also a genius.

Elephants with Beards:[1]
The Enigma of Wyndham Lewis

As I have already reported, I became an inhabitant of the Fitzroy Quarter of Tottenham Court Road after leaving the Slade. I found this district sympathetic, with its varied foreign population, its numerous cheap studios and restaurants and distinguished artistic traditions. (These remarks, except for the last, no longer apply.)

Wyndham Lewis, a later Slade student, also lodged here for some time. Somehow we came together and established a friendship which lasted on and off for a lifetime, with of course a good many long and salutary breaks.

His studio was in Charlotte Street, like mine. One entered it to find oneself up to one's knees in wastepaper: at that time he was composing sonnets in the Shakespearian form but of a more than Shakespearian obscurity. He seemed to be suffering from a form of verbal constipation which made it practically impossible for him to express himself in plain language, and this condition became still more marked in his handwriting, which was so squeezed and tortured in style as to be often quite illegible.

Not that he was constitutionally tongue-tied: indeed, when it came to assessing the shortcomings of his contemporaries he could be quite fluent. He had a particularly sharp eye for other people's physical defects, and was fully conscious of his own (for instance, he once, with unusual simplicity, confided to me his dissatisfaction with his *nose*). He was no athlete and admitted envying me my swimming accomplishment; he, too, would have liked to swim, but made no effort to learn. He was certainly interested in girls, but he found himself no match for their back-chat – I refer to the

[1] First published in *The Sunday Times* Magazine Section on October 5th, 1958.

factory girls we sometimes tried to consort with as potential models. His own rather recondite style of humour was wasted on them or answered in a spirit of levity which would have made Rabelais blush.

The advent of Dostoievsky on our consciousness was an important event about this time. In spite of a bad French translation, we both succumbed to these nightmare-like dramas of the soul, with their interludes of almost Dickensian absurdity. Turgenev was put aside (but in my case, at least, only for the time being). But to complicate matters, Nietzsche next appeared on the scene with the impact of a home-made bomb, scattering everybody and forcing even Dostoievsky to a secure but secondary eminence. Baudelaire alone remained immovable, as I suppose he still does; that old *marchand de nuages* is not easily dislodged ...

Surrounded spiritually by such a team of intellectual topnotchers, Lewis found himself in a serious predicament. Where did *he* come in? That was the question. First of all, for a start, he must drop Ingres. Didn't he, Lewis, have more than a talent for draughtsmanship himself? This Beauty stuff was overdone – no! *sarcasm*, with daring touches of scurrility, was to be his strong card. Hadn't Yeats hailed him as a second Swift? There was an opening here: in fact, life was full of openings, if you kept your eyes open.

But no truck with the proletariat! Shaw and others had pretty well exhausted that line, which in any case didn't attract P.W.L. in the least. There was no money in it.

About the time I have in mind we both made a change of address; Lewis found a studio somewhere in the Hampstead region and I in a street off the Marylebone Road. Visiting him one day I found him in his usual squalor, but I was surprised to note upon his desk a number of drawings of elephants. They were not ordinary elephants: *these elephants had beards*!

Expressing my astonishment, I taxed him with inconsistency: 'Elephants,' I said tentatively, 'do not, as far as I know, grow beards.' But Lewis, brushing me aside, answered rather sharply, 'You may be right, but I happen to *like* beards.' This was un-answerable, and I made no further cavil, zoological or otherwise, for I knew it was not a bit of good arguing with P.W.L. over questions of fact during one of his creative moods.

A similar *impasse* occurred during a show of his work arranged in her house by the amiable Lady Drogheda. Among the exhibits, hung a picture described as a portrait. Although taken from the back, the artist had included an attractive pair of breasts, ap-parently attached to the subject's shoulder-blades! (Was this the origin of Surrealism?) I thought it was going too far myself but, wisely, I think, made no comment. After all, I might have been mistaken. What I took to be the lady's back hair might have been her face in shadow or something; you never can tell.

When Lewis started his campaign of serious self-advertisement with his magazine *Blast* he made some important changes in his get-up at the same time; for a start, he had his hair cut. Up till then he had worn it long like any old Baroque artist, and his clothes were none too tidy. Now he smartened up a bit, for he was out for Big Business and no nonsense. As may be remem-bered by a few survivors of the period, he collected a small group of stalwarts round him, including the only incurable cubist in London; I refer to the gifted William Roberts, of course.

Under a banner with a strange device, 'The Vortex', these heroes conspired to overthrow one or two minor notabilities in the world of art, such as Henry Tonks of the Slade and Roger Fry, the Cézannist. Both these doctrinaires believed in cultivating the Old Masters – a thing which at that time was simply not done!

Roger Fry, an emancipated Quaker, became quite learned in this department of aesthetics, and for a start set up a pottery, dangerously near the headquarters of the Vorticists. Later he shifted his forces to the other side of the Tottenham Court Road, to blossom out eventually as the 'Bloomsburyites', with Clive Bell as their open mouthpiece, emitting tirelessly his brand-new slogan, Significant Form, where as a matter of fact neither form nor meaning was to be discovered!

Although Lewis was, of course, fully conscious of the importance of the Old Masters, he regarded them, I think, with some suspicion, as possible rivals. He wanted no competition from this quarter, though in the world of ideas he feared no rival – at least, not on this side of the Channel. In a word, his career must come first, but once *arrivé* he could afford, perhaps, to be less exclusive.

First of all, there were certain elements like Tonks and Fry and now Clive Bell to be liquidated. Others, on the other hand, were to be courted like Lord Beaverbrook or even Will Rothenstein, who without being great himself appeared to be on close terms with the Almighty.

And then there were *women*. As a student of Stendhal he was theoretically well versed in the technique of seduction as illustrated by that author, and the attitude of respectful servility he adopted in the presence of a beautiful woman of title might have been a useful gambit in the days of Julien Sorel, but seemed to me, and I think to the ladies too, a bit overdone in ours.

But Lewis was in favour of over-acting, for the truth is his view of life was based largely on the Commedia dell'Arte, a theatrical performance where everyone was allowed to invent his own gags or *lazzi*, and, provided he stuck to his role, could over-act as much as he liked, like clowns, who are, of course, in line with that incomparable tradition, the oldest in the world!

Unfortunately, he was a shy man and therefore could not himself take the lead in organizing a revival of this popular art; but how he revelled in any heaven-sent amateur of the tradition who might from time to time appear on the scene with his bag of tricks! Watching such performances attentively, he would applaud the miming, the postures and the bawdy witticisms, till, overcome with satisfaction, he would drop his mask and howl with laughter like a human being!

But it was the adherence to, even more than the deviations from, the norm which intrigued him most. This tendency is well illustrated by the admirable series of 'Tyros' in *Blast*. In these he presented a number of specimens of human fauna which were so closely related in form, teeth and colouring as to constitute what was practically a separate species, and which, though common as dirt, had never before been catalogued by science ...

Again, the Hell of Lewis's great trilogy is largely populated by crowds of indistinguishable ghosts who move about in concert, like bugs. Even the politicians who control them are easily recognizable types such as one sees by the score on any railway station here or on the Continent. Lewis was certainly a great anthropologist, but one who concerned himself not so much with *primitives* as with the people next door. It was for this reason, probably, that he frequented boarding-houses, preferably Polish ones, where he could study these highly undifferentiated nationals at his leisure.

In course of time my regard for Lewis suffered many setbacks, as his *pose* became more and more accentuated. This pose was composite, being based on several diverse models. After his return from the U.S.A. the conception of a 'Tycoon' or 'Big Shot' held pride of place in his repertoire, although the necessary accompaniment of dollars had been over-looked (I noticed with some anxiety). On a higher level still, Zarathustra himself was more than hinted at, though Lewis did not follow this lead to the heights of sublimity associated with that name; and then there was Baudelaire, of course, always good for a note of sombre disillusionment and misanthropy.

This mixture did not suit me at all. It was too strong for one thing, and I found it both unappetizing and repetitive.

But were these disguises really necessary? I asked myself. Was

Lewis a fugitive of some sort? But who on earth was after him?
I had never heard that he had ever been (like me) locked up. No,
I decided: such behaviour could only be the desperate stratagems
of an incurable Romantic *in flight from himself*!

This was the grand secret he had to keep or at least partly keep,
for he *enjoyed* being under suspicion, and would have loathed to
be placed in any known category by a psychiatrist or even a
policeman. After all, who could know better than himself what
was wrong – or right – with him? To be understood at all, there
lay the danger!

After the calamity to his sight, living as I did in the country,
I saw little of my old friend 'The Enemy', but would get him out
to dinner on occasions when I was visiting London. I made a
point of engaging some young female to join us, preferably a
handsome Scandinavian or a nice middle-European girl I knew,
as I had noticed my guest enjoyed the proximity of both and
preferred to hear an honest foreign accent rather than the hideous
vocables of the pseudo-genteel sub-dialect now cultivated in this
country by all classes. Besides, the stricken man was grateful for
a helping hand with his cutlery, etc. (His gastronomical tastes
remained simple and conservative to the end: soup, a mutton chop
or two followed by a trifle or an ice was all he asked for with his
champagne.)

He still wrote, I knew; and when first I heard of his calamity
I had wired him to bear up and above all stick to his art-criticism!
This impertinence was received, as I had expected, with complete
equanimity: he even seemed slightly amused. *Never once, during
our subsequent meetings, did my afflicted friend allude to the disaster.*
Instead of souring his spirit it seemed rather to have sweetened it.

The heart which he had so successfully disciplined was now
allowed to make its appearance at moments, though never
vocally. Lewis was incapable of pathos, and practised to the end
the reserve of a philosopher.

But now the game was up. No more delusions of power or Big Business; art politics were at an end for W.L. Art itself was out of sight, but, as it seemed to me, the humanistic basis of art, of which he had ever fought shy, now reasserted its gentler dominion over the fallen warrior who, wounded unto death, and now miles beyond questions of visibility – and of everything else – died, without recrimination or complaint, an Artist, if not a Hero, to the end.

The Flaming Terrapin:
Roy Campbell—Poet from South Africa

I WAS sitting in the old Café Royal one evening with Thomas Wade Earp, whose acquaintance I had lately made. He told me his friend Roy Campbell was due to join us shortly. Earp, or Tommy as I soon learnt to call him, was at that time at Oxford, where he held the distinguished position of President of the Oxford Union. He spoke of his friend. The young man was, I gathered, quite wonderful, not only good-looking but a poet of the highest promise ...

Presently the prodigy arrived. He was certainly a fine, tall young fellow with a careless buccaneer air about him which contrasted sharply with Tommy's cultivated precision of speech and manner. I took to him at once.

He hailed, it seemed, from South Africa, having been born and raised at Durban. He spoke in rather a high-pitched but not effeminate voice, occasionally employing the *click* characteristic of the Zulu language. Not once could one detect a trace of the famous accent of which Tommy Earp was, perhaps, barring one or two bishops, the sole exponent.

Sent Himself Down

Wyndham Lewis, with his acute powers of denigration, once described Roy Campbell's speech as resembling the call of an owl: not the screech-owl of course, but more the barn-owl variety – a kind of *hoot*. Roy had large misty eyes, directed, I noticed, quite frequently towards the tall rococo mirrors of the Café, in which, given a favourable angle, one saw oneself reflected to some

---

[1] First published in *The Sunday Times* Magazine Section on October 12th, 1958.

advantage. Tommy, as usual, was right; Roy Campbell was undoubtedly a good-looker, though not otherwise, perhaps, up to the standard of Moss Brothers Ltd.

I gathered from my first meeting with the young South African that, far from succumbing to the glamour of university life, he had reacted most unfavourably to it, and, with that touch of violence which we were to recognize in due course as the *leit-motiv* of his career, had, in despair, taken to the bottle in a big way as a means of counteracting the almost pathological condition of moral discomfort with which he had been troubled during his sojourn in our oldest seat of learning. At last, finding this situation intolerable, he decided to put an end to it, and without waiting for the formal dismissal, which no doubt was to be expected, he stole a march on the authorities and sent himself down.

Though Tommy may have been a little bit shocked by this behaviour, I was delighted myself, for in a sense Roy was now in my power. Being professionally an opportunist, I seized my chance and without any difficulty got him to sit for me at Mallord Street. The portrait, having been exposed in London where it excited no comment, eventually found its way to the United States (the nursery of many a good ugly duckling).

Masquerade

Having taken a house in Dorset at this time, I invited Roy down to stay with us at Alderney Manor, and on one occasion he brought with him his fiancée Miss Garmon; a charming and beautiful girl. Trelawney Dayrell Reid, a character I have already sketched in another place, was present to lend a necessary touch of style to the party. It was he, if I remember, who proposed the play-acting we organized one evening to amuse the children. This took the form of a kind of masquerade designed to celebrate the engagement of Roy Campbell and Miss Garmon. Trelawney himself took the role of the priest, for which he was admirably equipped, and Tommy Earp made a very good choir-boy, while I pretended to be an acolyte or something. It was good fun and I thought wanted very little to make it a true and valid ceremony. As a matter of fact, there could have existed no closer union in the world than that of Roy and Mary Campbell.

Wiping the Sword

Our next memorable meeting-place was at Martigues, where Roy and his family abode some years. But this, again, I have alluded to somewhere else. Afterwards, I regret to say, I saw but little of Roy, though I read what from time to time appeared of his poems and prose. We did meet now and then in London by accident during and after the Spanish Civil War, in which he claimed to have taken an important part; but I never took such pretensions very seriously. It was understood among us that Roy, however fine a poet, failed conspicuously when it came to faithful *reportage*; but nobody minded that – nobody who knew him, that is.

His vaunted prowess in the bull-ring seems to have passed unnoticed except by himself, though the *aficionados* are quick enough to acclaim valour when they see it. He may have joined in the *défilé* on horseback with his two little daughters, but the photograph he sent me of this feat showed, of course, no sign of a bull. At Martigues, indeed, he had indulged in the local sport of cow-baiting, and was, I believe, once knocked over by an irate milker whose new-born calf he was unsuccessfully attempting to skewer, but he never won a rosette or we'd have seen it displayed in Chelsea.

In his last book he had the impudence to vilify the brave *Anarqhistas* under Dureuti, who, armed with *sticks and stones only*, put Franco to flight at last, and would have settled his hash once and for all but for the intervention of Italian and Moorish troops and German planes, and the treachery of the Moscow-inspired 'Communists' in Barcelona.

But it is in his lofty scorn for the Gypsies that Roy Campbell reaches the nadir of venom. Why these people, after centuries of bestial persecution, should feel inspired to fight for anyone but themselves is beyond imagination! Here our Poet has sunk to the level of a public executioner, and he actually 'laughs' as he 'wipes his sword', stained with the blood of the poor, the innocent and the defenceless!

Regard Explained

How then, it will be asked, do I explain my continued regard for him? Well, I reply, for the reasons given already; I am not taken in by these purely literary exercises in bombast. I suspect this affectation of gigantic strength and ruthless courage. Vain as an exhibitionist child, he looks round for applause as he stretches out his hands for the baubles allotted to the prettiest, cleverest and bravest little man in the nursery.

In his last book, *Portugal*, Campbell proves himself to be a conscientious and thorough student of the literature of the country where he finally established himself. In numerous translations he manages to convey the diversity, charm and depth of a great poetic heritage which has by no means dried up and in which he seems to wallow luxuriously.

I, for one, do not find a similar wealth of sensibility in his own interminable effusions, of which the unceasing grandiloquence soon exhausts the reader, often causing him to turn with relief to the limericks, where our author's verbal facility is necessarily curbed in the harness of a more exacting form, but where he can still find room for the corrosive banter which came so naturally to him.

In this book on Portugal, Campbell, somewhat grudgingly, makes the *amende honorable* to the despised Gypsies, who after all, he admits, are the principal purveyors, if not indeed the originators, of the *fado*, that national instrument for the expression of a fundamental melancholy, the *cri de cœur* of the unloved!

Groaning Unheard

Nothing, however, to my mind, that he finds in his rummagings in the Portuguese treasure-house equals in beauty, depth and passion his versions after St Juan de la Cruz; but these, I cannot but think, are masterpieces in their own right. I think it must be to Campbell, too, that we owe the discovery of modern novelist, Eça da Queiros, two of whose admirable books he has translated.

The abject servility of his references to Salazar must disgust all but those who are blinded by religious prejudice; according to better historians than himself the stench of the poorer quarters of Lisbon, during what Campbell calls her Third Renaissance under its dictator, rises to heaven, but none may hear the groans of the unfortunates who languish in the filth of medieval dungeons without trial or hope.

Here, lest I be judged irreverent or unfriendly, I will borrow a few words from Roy Campbell himself and 'take my leave hoping I have given them a laugh or two (because that is partly what life seems to be for!). But also there is plenty of room for thanks, wonder and admiration' – and, I may add, *love*.

Old Masters

THE aspiring student who thinks he may best find himself by pursuing the Old Masters, is in grave danger of losing sight of his guides as well as his goal. He must take his directions, as did his distinguished predecessors, from life itself. Fidelity to venerable traditions too consistently practised and for too long may rob him of his fire and end in impotence. The subtle magic of antiquity can induce a form of hypnosis from which there is no awakening. The conjuration of an illustrious name, instead of fortifying, may only corrupt the student's innocence and damp his courage so that he sinks into the false security of precedent and the second-hand. Danger, not safety, must be wooed. Blunt crudity is better than polite sophistication: as frankness is superior to innuendo, and rusticity to metropolitan *chichi*. Aesthetic considerations can be over done: unlike hair-dressers, we cannot all be concerned with beauty alone.

Beauty crops up anywhere: a divine accident, it depends on illumination chiefly. It is distributed at random among human beings; some are awarded more than their fair share, some less, and others none at all. But fortunately tastes differ, and, as Montaigne observed, there is no wench so homely but will find her gallant.

Homeliness, indeed, as Thoreau noted, is next to beauty and a very fine thing. Any good drawing-master will tell his pupils to go first for character, not beauty. Character, in the art school, seems to consist of deviation from the norm: that is, implying imperfection. Therefore, it follows that perfect beauty must be characterless, and when found in the female of our species, is always so described by the less well-favoured, who presumably are compensated by an extra allowance of brains. But brains, being invisible, can hardly interest the budding draughtsman, unless he practises abstraction, when direct observation may be dispensed with.

I was standing at the bar of a French club I know of, when finding myself next to two young gentlemen of serious aspect, I invited them to join me in a glass of wine, the unique form of refreshment offered at this establishment. This offer being accepted, we entered into conversation of a rather tentative kind; but I soon became aware that I was in the presence of a couple of Abstractionists, who, as I began at once to hope, could be led to reveal something of the principles underlying a cult to which I had to admit myself a stranger; though it is true I had more than once listened to the airy bellowings of my friend, Victor Passmore, on the same subject, without feeling any the wiser. With an eye to an opening and a chance of enlightenment, I ventured to introduce what I thought would be a non-controversial issue to start with. Would they, I asked, be prepared to accept the validity of the European tradition of painting, and recognize, for example, the pre-eminence of Rembrandt as a draughtsman? A pause followed. Then the elder of the two replied: 'No,' he said gravely, 'we cannot admit Rembrandt.' With that I realized my indiscretion, and bidding these gentlemen good night, withdrew.

How dark, how Rembrandtesque, the night seemed as I made my way home!

Rembrandt, like our Abstractionists, might as reasonably lay claim to a mystique of his own, and hold secrets incommunicable unless to the initiate. The miller's son, after a youth and middle-age of constant labour, success and even glory, crowned by a fashionable marriage, was to suffer a tragic change of fortune. With the death of Saskia, he entered on the latter period of abandonment and obscurity. His association with Hendrike Stoffels, the wife of a policeman, involved him in blackmail, bankruptcy and social ostracism.

I

True, he had fallen from grace, but he landed on his feet. In the Jewish quarter of Amsterdam he was to find in abundance every element of life his soul delighted in. In these shadowy purlieus, full of cries and movement, were to be plucked the finest flowers of poverty. There was music, too. Hark! Whence comes this chanting we hear, and this quavering melody with its continual drone? It is the hurdy-gurdy man who slowly approaches with his talented family. There is his old wife and their handsome daughter who sings, the young girl who dances, the boy acrobat, the negro in faded splendour who plays the clown, quite a little troupe!

We are not alone in stopping to watch the strollers. Half-hidden in a doorway stands a robust figure with grey curls under an ancient hat. This man is sketching intently. It must surely be Rembrandt himself. Yes, there can be no doubt about it, it is Rembrandt van Ryn! But how different a Rembrandt from the one we knew from the pictures seen at Yan Six's house! Gone are the fine clothes, the feathers, the armour, the gold chain; all the swagger gone. Can this really be Rembrandt, this poor old man in rags ... ?

Dionysian Fury

IT MUST be admitted that there are times when the bright crown
of modesty (the glory and the despair of youth), with every rule
of decency on which we English are taught to build our lives,
must be cast aside and flouted at the call of a greater and a more
mysterious necessity. He who hears that call can have no choice
but to surrender. At once abandoning the allegiances of custom
with all their hallowed subterfuges, he strips himself and – dances!
He is enraptured: he is intoxicated: he is free! For the voice
he heard was a divine voice such as was listened to of old,
when men and gods were accustomed to meet on a more
reasonable and, I think, a more congenial footing than is now
usual.

I am no theologian, but I am by nature inclined to dispute the
wisdom of those grave myth-makers who refuse their pantheon
to all but one divinity. As far as the gods go, I confess myself a
pluralist, though holding them, like earthly monarchs, to be all
the better for careful limitation. No totalitarian! Even Christian
theology, somewhat grudgingly, admits three, or, including the
Virgin Mother, four members of the ruling Family, without
counting Lucifer of course, while at the same time insisting on
the essential singularity of all together. Such scholastic subtlety
is too fine for some of us, and leads inevitably to argument or
worse.

These reflections should be taken only as an introduction to a
type of so-called supernatural experience met with chiefly in
adolescence, but capable in some aspect of recurrence in maturity
or even old age. It may be called the *Dionysian Fury*, and under
that title will ordinarily manifest itself in the form of a gratuitous
and ecstatic dance. On one such visitation which I remember

pretty clearly, though it is far from recent, I was most inappropriately seized and possessed by the irresistible urge, while taking part in a formal promenade with my schoolfellows under the surveillance of our Headmaster. This inconsequence is the despair of philosophers and cannot be defended. I can only protest that in my case it was not induced by Art or favoured by precedent. Innocent (and ignorant) as I was, it took me by surprise: as it did my audience, apparently. The sun at least seemed to shine approvingly, and the sea to turn a deeper blue, as, throwing off my detested garments, I capered upon the shore as David might have danced before the Ark! My notions, if unrehearsed and wild, were, I am sure, no less vigorous than the Psalmist's, while developing, I seem to remember, an almost hieratic character, particularly as in my temerity I approached the Head. This tendency must have been instinctive, since my performance, I repeat, was quite impromptu. I found myself in a word 'full of the God', though I swear I had drunk nothing stronger than cocoa that morning. Meanwhile my schoolfellows, completely uninspired, looked on in wonder, and so did Mr Evans; but in his case wonderment was mixed, it seemed to me, with perplexity, and something else too: could it be *alarm*? Perhaps some long-forgotten impressions left over from a too cursory acquaintance with the classics now rose to the surface to bother him again and undermine his judgment. After all, wasn't he an M.A. or something? Anyhow, I suffered no penalty, nor even a reproof, for this indiscipline, though my reputation had already declined since the ex-policeman had on one occasion confiscated my drawings.

From now on the quality of the relationship subsisting between the Headmaster and myself began noticeably to deteriorate: the charming, humorous and idyllic misunderstanding I had so prized was foregone, to be succeeded by suspicion and even blunt antagonism on the one side, with bewilderment and disillusion on the other. My idol turned out to be of clay, according to its nature rapidly disintegrating before my eyes, with its beautiful mask (which I had provided) fallen to reveal the sad reality underneath. I have recorded elsewhere[1] the conclusion of this unfortunate affair (if that is the right word for it).

[1] *Chiaroscuro*, vol. I, p. 37.

The Prado Revisited, 1954

El Greco

Two gigantic old gentlemen, lightly clad in paper dressing-gowns, trip buoyantly in a landscape of cork and bottle-green, under the illumination of a gibbous moon which shines balefully between the incandescent shuttle-cocks of a sky in uproar. To judge by the mawkish satisfaction on the Saints' faces, they have at last hit upon the secret of accommodating logic and dogma, while making use of the same digital contortions as invariably accompany their inquiries into the relationship presumed to subsist between Aristotle and Holy Writ, or indeed any other dichotomy.

The Artist with his aversion from daylight and the commonplace, and his pious horror of sex, encloses himself in a dark box, peopled by manikins of his own invention who move like ghosts under the fitful gleams of a candle. Here he finds his freedom, as, luxuriating in his unparalleled rhythmic sense, he manipulates the distracted creatures, detaching them from the flames which they resemble, to bow in stark abjection before the blessed Intermediary, who, himself half-human, raises piteous eyes towards the majestic but yet benevolent looking Occupants of the *Gloria*.

Velasquez

This perfectly normal painter, with a more than normal mastery of his tools, surpasses himself with his little Infanta, who, in her way, is as great as Olivarez on Horseback. This painting of a plain child in her official finery defies description. Without its faultless colouration it would still be too clever by half. But, what an eye!

In the Lanzas the artist shows the finest sensibility and the most

134

delicate dramatic sense in portraying the exquisite courtesy of the victor, as, with a gentle smile, he lays his hand reassuringly and almost apologetically on the bowed shoulder of his defeated comrade-in-arms, who with equal grace and no less modesty proffers an unstained sword.

Goya

Leaving the age of the *hidalgo* and good-breeding, we come down with a leap into an epoch of vulgarity, brutality and witch-craft; an epoch which precedes our own more scientific, more universal ignominy. The French Revolution, like all revolutions, had betrayed itself, leaving behind human elements of incalculable grandeur, mixed with and over-ridden by the blood-thirsty pro-tagonists of Power. But a new political entity has arisen, that of *The People*. This cannot now be displaced but it can be circum-vented and utilized by cunning and trickery. The people ask for it: they seem born to be bamboozled. They even breed their own tyrants if necessary, for tyrants are always in demand, since they always come bearing gifts, which unfortunately have to be paid for by the recipients later on and with interest.

Francisco Goya y Lucientes, in spite of his grand name, was a man of the people, but he also became Court Painter, for there was no doubt about his supremacy, and he must have been personally irresistible. At that time photography hadn't begun to debauch people's powers of observation, nor were their minds yet befuddled by the abracadabra of literary pundits to which we are now beginning to be quite accustomed and may ignore. Students, condemned to the routine of State schools, weren't switched over to the study of 'Abstraction on Tuesdays'. There weren't any State schools. Goya, like everybody else in those days, learnt painting from a master, whose daughter, so as to be in a good tradition, he married. His portrait of his father-in-law is surely one of the best portraits in the world; even Gainsborough never did better, or so well. Gainsborough just lacked Goya's guts. Perhaps, like most Englishmen, he wasn't quite serious, and with all his fine sensibility, just a bit too easy-going. He could never approach Goya's 'Queen Marie-Louisa on Horseback'. This immense canvas is magnificent and disturbing. It beats Velasquez's similar arrangement of another royal equestrienne. He, Goya, wasn't overawed by his model, nor did he seek to flatter her. On the contrary, he saw her possibilities and enjoyed them. In spite of a strain of vulgarity she has an air ... slightly sinister perhaps, slightly *canaille*, but definitely not insignificant, and on this occasion even stately, like her horse ...

Goya, no doubt conventionally polite, was, it appears, too outspoken at times: he didn't disguise his sympathies for the poor, the outraged and the reviled. This sort of thing didn't do with his Royal Family, and when exiled in Bordeaux, he simply went on painting and drawing, just as if nothing had happened. *Aficionado* born and bred, he never forgot the bull-ring, as his late *Tauromaquia* testify, and probably had nothing to regret, except his inability to join in his favourite diversion any more. But he was never too old to paint.

A Visit from the King of Spain

'Du sang, de la volupté et de la mort.'

IT WAS during a showing of my pictures at the Chenil Galleries, Chelsea, now extinct. This institution, as it might be called, had arisen on the site of some studios I used to occupy between the Town Hall and the Six Bells Tavern. It consisted of picture galleries, a shop for artists' materials, and a projected restaurant. The aim of the founder, John Knewstub, had been to provide a cultural centre in a district long famous for its artistic and literary associations.

Although this ambitious project came to grief, several notable exhibitions and concerts were held before its eventual collapse. The restaurant, however, never materialized, and if the kitchen, which occupied the most important position on the frontage, was of a capacity to meet the requirements of a regiment, it was never, as far as I know, productive of so much as a boiled egg. The distinguished architect, George Kennedy, who is to be held responsible for this anomaly, must have suffered partial paralysis while under the influence of the megalomaniac it was his fate to collaborate with. If so, he wasn't the only one to wilt under the persuasive oratory of the founder, who, when words failed him, as they often did, was in the habit of replacing them by an even more meaningful silence, accompanied by an expression of mystic rapture acquired in the neighbouring tavern, and more effective even than the longest words his vocabulary might have furnished when in working order. In these circumstances Knewstub's two distinguished brothers-in-law, Orpen and Will Rothenstein, agreed for once in maintaining an attitude of strict neutrality, not to say aloofness, which was a pity, as such a combination of financial solvency and spiritual illumination would have supplied

137

all that was necessary to the successful launching of the concern. As it was, its begetter mostly had to rely on the co-operation of strangers, who, as a matter of fact, with less réclame and no matrimonial claims, proved better sportsmen.

Thus the building proceeded, though precariously, by fits and starts. The foundation stone at any rate was well and truly laid as I saw for myself; but one indispensable factor of success was missing – no life was lost in the building operations! No corpse could be adduced to guarantee the protective agency of a domestic ghost: nobody even had been hurt! As any mason knows, such immunity can only be purchased at the price of good luck. And although some coins bearing the image of the reigning sovereign were included in the foundation ceremony, these after all amounted only to a convenient substitute for a purer and more effective sacrifice. Blood, and blood only, has always been held to be the necessary adjunct of salvation, and there were found individuals among the more generous supporters of the enterprise, who, later on, were heard to express the view that, *faute de mieux*, Knewstub himself might very fittingly have been offered up on his own altar. However this may be, some successful exhibitions and concerts were organized before the debacle, and are to be credited to Knewstub's zeal and vision. It was here that John Barbirolli made his debut, and here that I once trod on the toes of Vaughan Williams, who, like myself, was at the moment wholly absorbed in the songs of Philip Heseltine as interpreted by an attractive soprano. For this *faux pas* I incurred the expostulations of the Master, who received my apologies so kindly as to make him my friend as well as his admirer for life.

It was here, too, that a show of my paintings provided the occasion to which the heading to this note refers, and for which a friend at Court, as good-natured as she is beautiful, was responsible. After examining my efforts King Alfonso expressed a wish to visit my studio in Mallord Street, and, a taxi being found, we all drove thither. I was quite ready for some refreshment and I think so were my guests, for compliments, even when sincere, can be tiring in the long run, to the maker and to the recipient, and a change of subject becomes a necessity. The conversation turning to bull-fighting, the King said that although he considered himself 'the first Spanish man' and as such compelled by ceremony to attend the *corrida* on occasions, he did not approve of this national mania, for it reflected unwholesomely on the Spanish character and reputation. 'Foreigners,' he said, 'are apt to think us barbarians. But,' he added, 'this form of sport cannot continue much longer, for such is the enormous number of old horses killed in the arena on Sundays throughout Spain that even these wretched and decrepit creatures are becoming alarmingly scarce and costly.' This observation was made before the present practice of providing protective quilts came into force, an innovation which certainly prolongs the life of the animal while, of course, reducing its value in the market. No sign is to be remarked yet of any diminution in popularity of this game or ritual. The arenas are still packed to the sky-line and the cult of valour, skill and grace still holds the field in a country where the imminence of Death is accepted as the irremediable corollary of Beauty, Power and Love. This folk-drama is of the people, and it is at once gay, elegant and grotesque. The Beast is always slain and sometimes the Hero, too. There is no betting.

Before parting, the King astonished me by confessing his inability to make me his Court Painter, much as he would like to. To appoint a foreigner to this office, he explained, would seriously endanger his popularity and would be certainly opposed by his Ministers: he would however be glad to sit for me sometime in Madrid. The possibility of such a development had never occurred to me, except perhaps as a joke, but it was the result of the generous impulses of Lady Irene, my charming intermediary in this encounter with a most sympathetic Monarch.

Notes from Hospital

IN SPITE of the general debasement of taste and manners in this age; in spite of the cult of uniformity and the substitution of the polling-booth for the mote and the Witenagemote, with the delegation of authority to professional spell-binders at Westminster, and the resultant stultification of the electorate; in spite of the new journalism, with its indifference to truth and its venal plugging of the sensational; in spite of the ever-widening gulf between the professional and the wage-earning classes; in spite of the decay of popular handicrafts, the vulgarization of science and the abuse of machinery; in spite of the ruination of our coastal scenery by the military and the desecration of high places by misguided engineers; in spite of everything in fact which distinguishes this New Elizabethan Age, are we to submit, to be stunned into acquiescence by the hammer-blows of Big Business? Are we to connive at mass-cozenage and the suppression of the politically powerless? Are we to strike our colours at the command of any majority? No, because our banner is sacred to the memory of the unconquerable dead, through whom reach us intimations of better things to come. But who are *we*? Well, there's myself and possibly somebody round the corner.

El Dorado
The poor are always with us. Fortunately; for after all it is they who provide the millions.

Noblesse Oblige
Every Englishman loves a Lord: starting with Our Lord Jesus Christ, of course.

* * *

Despairingly, I enter a certain restaurant club in the King's Road, Chelsea. The hour is unfashionable, the bar empty. I order a fiasco of Chianti. A pretty Italian girl serves me, and, with a roguish smile, remarks: 'S'nice to sit down with a good drink and enjoy yourself, isn't it?'

*　　*　　*

Among the Gypsy Coppersmiths I met in Italy, I found to my astonishment some friends I had met at Cherbourg two or three years before. These consisted of a young man, his very handsome wife and some children. We were seated in their tent and were drinking wine. Recollecting a song I had learnt in earlier days, I proceeded to repeat these verses, which were of an amorous nature, and included a line I would have done well to omit, a line I regret to say of the greatest indecency. Carried away by the lilt of the melody, however, and heedless of the sense of the words, I failed to arrest myself in time, and the extreme embarrassment of my audience which followed convicted me of a serious breach of the proprieties. It took considerably more than another bottle to restore our equanimity. These are the offending words. I do not propose to translate them: '*Spivado ančo mui o Kar.*'

*　　*　　*

The sense of modesty quickly disappears in a nursing home. The patient soon submits to the closest inspection without a qualm, and as for the nurses, their professional training admits of no squeamishness, though it by no means excludes the genial byplay appropriate to youth and good looks. The discovery that nudity is neither erotic nor shameful permits one to ignore the taboos without danger or discomfort.

The young nurses who keep passing across the square opposite are rather fascinating. They wear triangular white caps, like those so fashionable among the male inhabitants of Tierra del Fuego. Their little black capes are worn so that they appear to have no arms. Their legs are enshrouded in blue skirts and they wear white aprons. I see everything double, which adds to the strangeness of the scene. They remind me of old-fashioned paupers out for exercise. There are green lawns and some tall plane trees painted in the Pointilliste manner of Seurat. Often a tall black student walks past, with an open book in his hand and an air of abstraction.

* * *

Although, in the past, a great frequenter of Gypsies, I have painted but few, so fascinated have I been in their society that I have always felt loth to set about operations on the spot. It would have broken the spell. However, I have sometimes lured individuals among them to sit for me, and have in some cases been able to reconstruct whole groups from memory and without much difficulty. One such composition, life-size and containing scores of figures – Coppersmiths met with in Italy – was bought by Horace Cole, the practical joker. Later, repenting of this deal, I bought it back and then sold it to a Japanese collector for three times its former price. Cole was much annoyed when he heard this.

* * *

Propinquity is the greatest of stimulants. It may lead to love or murder; like a bottle of wine within reach, it can provoke both thirst and nausea, according to the label and the state of our stomachs, but never indifference.

* * *

The painted tombs of Etruria, the gay Minoan palaces, the stately towers of Mycene, all these compel our admiration and envy, but the attractions of the Misses Tickell at Dulwich are, for me, just as valid, and, being so accessible, warmer.

The Greatest Repartee in History

Paris. A café on the right bank. Oscar Wilde among the company, which includes also a youngish writer then to the fore called Ernest la Jeunesse. This writer was in the habit of illustrating his books, not with drawings, but with snapshots of his characters in action. He was regarded as a mysterious figure and spoke in a piercing falsetto. After a while he left us and Oscar told the following story:

'Everybody,' he said, 'used to wonder what could account for this man's extraordinary voice: could it be natural, a freak, or was it assumed? Well,' said O.W., 'once when this subject was under discussion, the publisher of La Jeunesse, who happened to be present, intervened. "There's no mystery about it," he announced, "my poor friend is completely impotent, and that's all there is to it." This crude statement was in due course reported to La Jeunesse, who, after giving it careful consideration, decided that he must do something about it. Such a remark was injurious, besides being in bad taste. His publisher, rich and powerful as he was, must be taught a lesson. After much thought, he finally devised a plan of action which would not only provide an adequate answer to the libel, but would at the same time illustrate those strict principles of ultra-realism to which he as an artist was committed. Since, according to his calculations, the success of his operations demanded the collaboration of a third party, who in fact had, necessarily, to be the publisher's wife herself, a lady not exactly young but of spotless reputation, the task our talented friend had set himself seemed indeed formidable. If, as the protagonist of a new iconoclasm, La Jeunesse could be imagined as bearing anything so trite as a banner, the device inscribed thereon, would, I fancy, take the form of a slogan much more homely and practical than *Excelsior*. However that may be, the young man set to work and though the siege was long and arduous, goodwill and tenacity prevailed as usual and the day arrived when, his honour vindicated and his manhood proved, the happy though somewhat exhausted warrior could sit back and relax in peaceful contemplation of his victory, and he, being by now, as you may guess, treated as a member of the family, was usually to be found in the neighbourhood of the *nursery*, whence the shrill cries of a lusty babe seemed, like his own penetrating treble, to proclaim the triumph of actuality and goodbye to dreams. Thus,' wound up Oscar, 'was contrived *The Greatest Repartee in History*.'

I have made no attempt, of course, to reproduce Oscar Wilde's narrative style in this excerpt from my memories of the great raconteur. I don't suppose the peculiar quality of his English could possibly be conveyed except by expert mimicry, nor could his French (also spoken with an Oxford accent) be reconstructed from memory or recorded by means of any known system of phonetics. In the former language he expressed himself through the medium of what was practically an artificial sub-dialect of his own invention, which has fortunately almost died out, since when employed by lesser wits it at once became an intolerable affectation. In the Master's own entourage, however, it was indispensable in those days, as it conferred upon its practitioners a certain *cachet* suggestive of a culture and breeding which, without it, might have passed unnoticed. This entourage, usually composed almost exclusively of snobs, lick-spittles, social hangers-on and crawlers-up, might sometimes include an artist or two of the school of Burne Jones, but in general would be about as sympathetic to a painter as an assemblage of church workers at the vicar's annual garden party. (But professional actors mustn't quarrel with their audiences.) The Reverend Oscar Wilde was always a cut above his company, for he had more wit and fun in him than all his parishioners combined, and more wisdom, too, if it comes to that, in spite of his occasional lapses in taste which were only in the spirit of the age after all, and more than matched in the music hall of his time. I cannot accept the mouldy old caution Lautrec made of him, sitting *alone* in the Folies Bergères, like a partly warmed-up corpse. (As if he ever sat *alone* anywhere!) There was nothing lugubrious or sinister about him. He fancied himself as a kind of Happy Prince, or, admitting a touch of vulgarity, the genial although permanently overdrawn millionaire, and if he suffered from the blues, sometimes, what could be more natural? With luck there would be Robbie Ross round the corner. 'Oh, Robbie, I've had such a *frightful* dream!' 'What was it, Oscar dearie?' 'I dreamt I was dining in H-H-Hell! Oh, Oh, Oh!' 'There, there, Oskywosky, but Robbie's sure you were the life and soul of the party.' In another mood. Will Rothenstein: 'But I sometimes feel so *ridiculous*, Oscar!' O.W. in a stage whisper, 'But, *of course*, my *dear* Will, didn't you *know*? *All real* artists *are* ridiculous!'

Yes, it was a bright spirit who passed away at the little Hotel d'Alsace near the Beaux Arts, where I used to stay myself, but without ever being inspired to make anything like so endearing and memorable an impression on the management as Oscar did when he blew up with such a lovely bang! What a brilliant idea! What a perfect exit! Though I never saw him as a young man myself, my memory of him isn't of a middle-aged man at all, but will always evoke the frank, open, friendly, humorous face of a young one, for the fact is he had too much sense to grow old, and wisely left that process with complete confidence to his detractors, his apologists and Mr Punch.

Communism

> 'And all that believed were together, and had all things common. And sold their possessions, and parted them to all men, as every man had need.' – Acts ii, 44–5.

THE above quotation will of course be familiar to Bible students. But as most people, like children, are apt to take their beliefs on trust, its republication at the present time may not be out of place. It affords unequivocal evidence of the kind of society recommended by the Apostles and practised by the Early Church, i.e. a form of Communism, in fact. I, and probably many others, have waited long and anxiously for a more authoritative reference to this important passage of the Scriptures, preferably emanating from the clergy, a bishop, or other competent source, together with an appropriate commentary, since the intrusion into such a field by a layman like myself might easily be dismissed as impertinent or pass unnoticed.

At a time when the forces of Christendom and Communism (of another variety) are mustering for the final struggle, it is above all necessary to avoid doctrinal hair-splitting and wholeheartedly to join forces under a single banner. It is a question of freedom or slavery, life or death, black or white. It is as simple as that: or is it?

But some of our scientific Jeremiahs warn us that the outcome of the coming test match can only be the disappearance of civilization itself, and with it the destruction of all values, including every monument to the spirit of man or the Glory of God raised by Art and Genius of the past down to those of our own day. Since these are irreplaceable, the fate of any possible human survivors is of no great consequence; in any case the results of the new weapons with their chemical concomitants will have completely dehumanized and distorted them beyond recognition or possibility of recovery.

But whatever the outcome of the grand catastrophe envisaged, the immediate cost of our preparations for it will soon lead to bankruptcy, and will never be met by our unfortunate descendants, who will have been forced to take refuge underground, where they will eke out the remainder of a precarious existence in darkness and a permanent state of insolvency. Such is the outlook.

To return to our document. We know already that the somewhat happy-go-lucky way of life briefly illustrated therein would be quite impracticable in any highly industrialized society such as ours, and that the law has provided severe deterrents to its practice. The sacredness of private property has always been the head-stone of civilized societies, and we can depend on our admirable police force to ensure its enforcement despite the aggression of thieves, murderers or even the subversive activities of Utopian doctrinaires; wandering and penniless agitators are not encouraged, and the dangerous experiments of Winstanley, Lilburne *et hoc genus omne* are not to be repeated with impunity now, any more than in the time of the Diggers. Although Cobbett might ride all over England on Common Land, it would be unwise to try that now. For one thing, there *is* no Common Land to speak of left. There is only the House of Commons to remind us of it. Along with the disappearance of this ancient institution, the march of progress has obliterated much of the engaging diversity of the old tribal life, such as we now look back upon with mild nostalgia, replacing it with a more manageable uniformity, dear to the hearts of our legislators, both central and local. If regional customs and costumes are now only fading memories, and the rustic dances and songs of our merrier ancestors are now enjoyed only in the inaccessible circles of learned dilettanti, have we not in compensation the boundless resources of wireless to draw upon, to fill our leisure and refresh our minds? And, as our indigenous culture recedes into the dim background of history, more up-to-date techniques of entertainment exported from the U.S.A. take its place. The heartrending ululations of the crooner have effectively silenced the voice of the turtle, and our intricate old dialects give way before the clipped vocables of a newer and smarter world. But stop! I am going too fast! The Lancashire accent still provides the most reliable medium for our best comedians, and an artificial sub-dialect of Cockney, only heard on the air, remains to this day the favourite instrument of our worst.

With these few exceptions, the North-Americanization of this and other countries proceeds apace, although it must be admitted the behaviour of the G.I.s when released from the restraints of their homeland leaves much to be desired. These wayward crusaders somehow fail to make themselves generally popular in Europe, and, unlike our own countrymen abroad, are only tolerated, rarely loved. Is this perhaps due to the fact that the great cultural stream, issuing from the Mediterranean Basin, has never washed the shores of the U.S.A.? Yet it appears to have been a 'Wop' who first gave his name to the country ... The later infusion of blood from Italy and other classic lands has not yet been thoroughly assimilated, unless in a few areas such as Chicago or Boston.

These gentle influences take time to make themselves felt; it is a nation in the boiling-pot we are considering, not the eventual Irish or other stew.

We are lucky indeed on this side in having the services of a Prime Minister [Churchill], himself a hybrid, whose acute and discerning mind will know how to provide the stepping-stones towards a fresh rapprochement. In the meanwhile, we may well for the time being waive our political differences in the contemplation of such exotic and endearing figures of recent memory, as, say, the incredible Mizners, the poet of the Sierras, Jaoquin Miller, or even, though perhaps with less unanimity, the graver personality of ex-Governor Fuller of Massachusetts, happily still at large. We have nothing comparable over here. But we cannot yet turn to our cousins overseas for help in the resolution of all our ideological problems, since their minds are for the moment fully occupied with the spectacular menace of a formidable Eurasian Power professing a brand of Communism as much at variance with the doctrines illustrated in our text, as it is with the Way of Life which both our peoples have since developed and apparently prefer. But the reiterated injunction of the Master, 'Feed my Sheep', in its simplicity will always appeal to me at least with greater force than the Marxian slogan, 'the Dictatorship of the Proletariat', with all the bloody methods of its attainment which we are familiar with. I myself dislike to be dictated to by anybody and am inclined, like Thucydides and others of his time, to be an *anarch*, or 'agin the Government' and the lust for, and abuse of, power which invariably goes with it. This brought ruin to ancient Greece and many other countries. It may do the same for ours.

In my view, the best way to combat error is first to ascertain the truth, and then tell it, even if this be risky. Those with a taste for heroism may easily indulge it without resorting to chemicals or guns. The use of napalm may, and indeed does, deprive your opponent of his flesh; it lays bare his bones, or turns his skin to 'crackling', but does it teach him his grammar? How is he to express himself intelligently in such circumstances? You will have left him unconvinced, painfully shy, and probably resentful. Such conduct is not cricket or even football, and should be eschewed.

Warfare, let us admit it, has now lost all its glamour. *La Gloire* is out of date, and, as all good soldiers know, the spectacle of terrified men clawing at each other's throats is by no means edifying. A better field for action, where courage, scientific resource and perhaps personal sacrifice is called for, can be found in our Dependencies overseas. The islands of the Antilles, which, like an exquisite necklace of pearls, enclose the blue Caribbean, are found upon exploration to reveal under British administration, coupled with the benevolent intervention of the United Fruit Co. Inc., anything but paradisaic conditions: disease is rife, squalor and slums abound, although the people are free – to vote as much as they like or even refrain altogether. It is only in Australia and the U.S.S.R. that this privilege has so far been made compulsory.

The unpleasant aspects of colonization may not immediately strike the tourist, who sticks to the beauty spots and the best hotels. He is out for a good time and no doubt gets it. He sees and perhaps admires the charming cabins of the islanders, roofed with palm and washed with pink and blue, gleaming like jewels amidst the iridescent verdure of an enchanted island, but he doesn't go too near. Instinctively he fights shy of poverty which always makes him feel uncomfortable and might mean a call upon his purse. 'Carry on, driver!' Writing home, he becomes quite literary: 'This isle is full of noises, sounds and sweet airs, which give delight and hurt not' (except for that God-damned piccaninny howling under my window, he murmurs in paren-thesis); and naturally he makes a point of mentioning 'the still-vext Bermoothes', even if he doesn't land on them. But Nassau he will love. Good society, good clubs, English peers, Indian maharanees in Parisian saris; good bathing and drinks; no economically-minded millionaires, no sign of Caliban, and, best of all, not one beauty spot to bother about.

But these digressions are not getting us much further in our inquiry. We are still faced with the original dilemma: the com-plete incompatibility of the two forms of Communism confront-ing us. They cannot both be valid, nor can they, as opposites, be equally bogus, but both offer alternatives to our present system, which, whatever its merits, is, as has been seen, doomed to disappear. For the first, the Apostolic order, we have in support the example afforded by primitive societies which without their communal basis could hardly have survived; these cultures, it is true, are now rapidly disappearing under the impact of civilizing agencies from Europe and the Far East. But unfortunately the appearance of the whites among a coloured population seems to have a lethal, or at least a stupefying, effect. For that matter, it has been known in some cases to produce similar results at home; but in the Pacific Islands, where whole populations have withered away before the White Man's fatal magic, it would seem better to have allowed such societies to flourish in their own way, though the newcomers, without forcible interference, might yet give them the benefit of a superior technology: their primitive methods of agriculture, for instance, are unsatisfactory, and their therapeutic practices inadequate, particularly when faced with the problems arising from contamination and epidemic disease. I am aware that much is now being done in this line, although a little late in the day, and usually in association with the imposition of less appropriate political conceptions, irrespective of tradition.

As for rival theologies, let us leave the gods to fight it out among themselves! The employment of penicillin requires no religious sanction. For 'savages', life is an elaborate game in which we can take no part. It involves outwitting the demoniacal powers by means of methods well within the compass of the shaman's or medicine-man's voluminous repertory. No spiritual dogmas need be insisted on by our protagonists, no conventions of imported propriety set up. Paganism, too, can boast her virtues, and even a pre-eminence of style, and, as in Art, two or more cultures have been known to associate without discord. Perhaps, indeed, the outcome of racial interfusion may lead to a happier form of society founded on freedom, understanding and good will; the resolution of all creeds and the eventual celebration of the Marriage of Heaven and Hell in a harmony undreamt of except by a few religious visionaries such as William Blake or Shelley. In such a happy denouement, even the mild injunctions of the Galilean might not be wholly ignored, but the Hegelian erection of an almighty police state would certainly find no support: we have seen too much of that. Man cannot surpass himself, but he can rise to an occasion, for his psychological make-up includes, besides his normal propensity to delusion, an equally fundamental capacity for hope.

Index

Index

Index